Working With Street Children

An Approach Explored

Andrew Williams

Un'
Ch
Subje

Russell House Publishing

First published in 2011 by:
Russell House Publishing Ltd.
58 Broad Street
Lyme Regis
Dorset DT7 3QF
Tel: 01297-443948
Fax: 01297-442722
e-mail: help@russellhouse.co.uk
www.russellhouse.co.uk

© Andrew Williams

British Library Cataloguing-in-publication Data:
A catalogue record for this book is available from the British Library.

ISBN: 978-1-905541-80-5

Typeset by TW Typesetting, Plymouth, Devon
Cover artwork by Bernie Georges
Cover design by Bernie Georges and Jeremy Spencer
Printed by Page Bros, Norwich

Russell House Publishing

Russell House Publishing aims to publish innovative and valuable materials to help managers, practitioners, trainers, educators and students.

Our full catalogue covers: families, children and young people; engagement and inclusion; drink, drugs and mental health; textbooks in youth work and social work; workforce development.

Full details can be found at www.russellhouse.co.uk
and we are pleased to send out information to you by post. Our contact details are on this page.

We are always keen to receive feedback on publications and new ideas for future projects.

Contents

Foreword

The Most Reverend and Right Honourable Dr John Sentamu, Archbishop of York

Growing up in Uganda I had the joy and privilege of growing up in a large family, with a father and mother, and I was one of thirteen children. We didn't have much by way of material possession but we knew we were loved and cared for, and we all looked out for each other. So reading stories of children as young as four or six being forced to leave home and live on the streets of any town or city is heart breaking.

Physiologists and psychologists tell that when the human body is under excessive stress, whether from internal worry or external circumstances, a bodily reaction is triggered called the "fight or flight response". This response is hard-wired in our brains and is designed to protect us from bodily harm. I want to thank God that when overwhelmed and faced with the challenges and acute needs he saw on the streets of Kampala, Andrew Williams could have taken the next flight out of Entebbe but he didn't. He chose to stay and fight and this book unearths the abundant harvest of his struggles.

Many of us hear and read about street children and simply log that information at the back of our minds as a statistic, quickly forgetting that they are someone's child and grandchild, niece or nephew, wonderfully and fearfully made in the image of God. These children are in a place where they should not normally be. They should be enjoying a loving and caring home where they are enabled to grow and flourish and enjoy being children.

To this end, I strongly commend this book to all practitioners, would-be practitioners, all decision makers and opinion formers to remind them and all of us that each story told in this book represents a real person and actual circumstances. I urge readers to do everything you can to help give these children a hope and a future. Be an agent of change and transformation in their precious God-given lives.

✝ Sentamu Ebor
Archbishop of York
England
July 2011

Preface

I wish this book did not exist because I wish street children did not exist! Anyone working on a daily basis with street children knows what I mean. The work may be worthwhile and at times rewarding but there is an ache, a discomfort working with young people who should never have been allowed to experience what most street children have. Yet the book does exist largely because five people – independently of each other and for different reasons – challenged me to write a book. It exists for anyone working with street children, for those thinking about working with children at risk, those managing people working with street children and anyone in a position of influence concerning the plight of street children.

> In the dead of night, my right knee pressed into Ronald's shoulder blade to enable me to lean across and push down hard on his other arm. He stared into my eyes with a look of desperation, unable to muster a sound as searing pain and panic set in. The doctor worked hard to save his life – and succeeded. He removed pieces of filthy, torn up tee-shirt embedded into a deep, gaping hole in Ronald's head. Other street children had stuffed them in, eager to stop the bleeding after four men attacked Ronald with pangas (machete style knives) and left him to die. There was no time for anaesthetic as fierce rigors indicated the onset of septicaemia. My job was to control Ronald's movement to allow the doctor to reopen the wound, remove dirt and begin treatment immediately. Ronald had been resistant to care and assistance offered and had caused many headaches (and would continue to do so) amongst the small but dedicated staff team. Yet none of that mattered. What mattered was his life.

In the heat of such moments – and there were many – we just got on with it. We didn't wonder about measuring impact or our strategic methodology. We didn't ponder how such responses were mere drops in the ocean. To do so would have been daft but even at less intense times, the demands and pressures of pioneering and initiating new work were so great that pausing to reflect on, articulate or document it was almost impossible. Despite that, we produced reams of discussion papers, dream plans, aims and objectives. This book brings together, concisely and retrospectively, the thinking and experience they represented. It offers a snapshot from history to explain what we did and why, the trials and triumphs, the lessons learned, the background and twelve year process which saw a vision become reality.

Retrak

In 1995, Paul Joynson-Hicks shared that vision with my wife, Katina, and I. He was living and working as a photographer in Kampala, Uganda. A year earlier, he had been challenged to respond to the growing number of children loitering day and night on Kampala's streets. After years of civil unrest, peace had come to Kampala and urban migration was on the increase.

Rather than accepting glib explanations for the presence of street children and their needs, Paul and a youth worker, Matt Winn, set about discovering more by setting up Tigers Football Club in October 1994. The number of boys attending increased, as did their demands for attention, assistance and opportunity. Discipline was a challenge. In order to develop and establish an organisation which built on the foundations of the football club and relationships formed with street children and key players in the community, full time directors were needed. Paul sought people with backgrounds in social work and education who had lived and worked in Africa. Our paths crossed in 1995. After much discussion, a feasibility visit to Kampala and raising support we relocated to Uganda the following year. Paul handed over leadership and I am indebted to him for his vision and courage. Also, to his family and friends, who like our own, gave sacrificially over many years to ensure street children were restored and empowered through the work of a sustainable social work organisation. As early as 1996, we cogitated about seeing the work expand throughout the continent of Africa. If the model worked, it must be shared. After nine years of planning, implementing, reviewing and reworking we were ready to do so. Plans to initiate new work in Ethiopia had already begun when, in 2005, the organisation was rebranded and officially launched as Retrak. Operations and a head office were set up in Kenya shortly afterwards.

This book

This book explores the approach which shaped and informed an organisation's birth and development. Current thinking and practice has built on that foundation in a way which corresponds to the book's message – we should continually review and critically self-reflect in order to improve our service delivery and increase our impact.

This book aims to improve the lives of street children in any part of the world by:

- Strengthening, equipping and encouraging those who work with and amongst street children.
- Inspiring and preparing some people to start working with street children.
- Urging others to act and advocate on behalf of street children.

Who might benefit from reading it?

The readers I have in mind are firstly, fellow practitioners. This book can be used for reference or in training either individually or in groups. I believe we can learn from each other irrespective of where we work even though culture and context are so critical. The practitioners I refer to are those who work directly with street children in a professional capacity. The terms 'social worker', 'relational worker' and 'key worker' are used interchangeably. There are no 'social workers' in some parts of the world, in other parts you can become one after a one-day workshop and in other countries it is a term reserved exclusively for those qualified and legally registered as such. The same can be said for youth workers and counsellors. This book is designed for those who have been given responsibility for the care, welfare, guidance and empowerment of individual street children and young people.

The second group of readers I have in mind are those who are considering working with street children or other groups of especially vulnerable children. You may already be training for work with children and young people in your own country or abroad. The anecdotes and illustrations offered provide an insight into the work and level of commitment it demands. If some people are put off working with street children by this book it will have achieved something. Such readers may not have fully appreciated all that is entailed. They may have been enabled to re-evaluate their own skills or motives in the light of what they read. For those who do pursue working with street children, the book may inspire you to access other resources available, to network more rigorously and learn from others. As a result, I pray that creative and innovative responses will develop which are contextually relevant and effective.

Thirdly, this book is written with decision makers and managers in mind. One reviewer expressed how he hopes directors and trustees of every street child organisation will read it. Knowing the field is essential for effective governance. Of course, no two organisations or contexts are the same but the book is one opportunity to learn what others have done and learnt by doing so. I hope that managers with responsibility for programmes or those mandated to work with street and homeless children will read this book for guidance and reference, to strengthen review and inform reflective practice.

People for whom this book will, I hope, be of interest also include those that support, have supported or will support, endeavours with street children. Some of our own supporters have not merely donated but have inspired, shaped, encouraged and visited. If that's you, please read on and as you do be, reminded of the impact your partnership made and continues to do so in the lives of those represented.

About the Author

Andrew Williams MBE MA MSc CQSW has twenty years experience of direct work with children and young people. He is co-founder, former CEO and President Emeritus of Retrak, an organisation widely respected for its work amongst street children in Africa. Andrew was born in Uganda, studied at Edinburgh University and for an MSc in Applied Social Studies at Oxford University before qualifying as a probation officer.

In 1996 Andrew and his wife, Katina, accepted an invitation from Uganda to develop a football club for street boys into a social work organisation. Retrak (formerly known as The Tigers Club Project) was registered in 1997. To widen impact and reflect significant changes, the charity was rebranded and officially launched as Retrak in 2005. Andrew relocated to Kenya to establish a head office in Nairobi and operations began in Ethiopia. In 2006, he was awarded the MBE for services to disadvantaged children in Uganda.

Andrew moved with his family to UK in 2008. He is a registered social worker and combines an acting career with consultancy, advocacy, training and support for child-focussed NGOs. He hopes this publication will contribute to fulfilling a vision of a world in which every child has dignity and opportunity and no child is forced to live on the street.

* * *

For further information about this and future publications or for details of training, consultancy and support services please visit www.workingwithstreetchildren.com. To contact the author directly email andrew.williams@workingwithstreetchildren.com.

To my family – Katina, Charlotte, Zak & Suzi –
whose life was joyfully entwined with Retrak for many years.
Thank you for immense support and sacrifices made.

In memory of Kapapa

Acknowledgements

I acknowledge and thank those involved in the process of writing this book; the five individuals who urged me to get writing; Steve Warner and Chris Start for moral support, wise counsel and technical expertise; Polly Maclachlan and Simon Cansdale who read draft manuscripts and gave critical feedback and were later joined by peers from social work and street child sectors including Mick Pease, Sarah Thomas de Benitez, Andy Sexton of the 180 Alliance, Sally Shire and others from Consortium for Street Children (CSC); Berni Georges for cover artwork; Martin Jones and Geoffrey Mann at Russell House for commitment, patience and advice; Archbishop John and Margaret Sentamu for years of interest, prayerful support and encouragement and for writing the foreword.

The journey with street children which informed and inspired this book was shared with many people. They include; Paul Joynson Hicks who imparted the vision and his sister Rowena who introduced us; Board members of Retrak led by Pat Davall, Colin Robinson, Karen Brown who brought unique and appropriate passion and skills; leaders, experts and co-workers we leaned on and learned from including Stuart Pascall, Hugh Osgood, Kenneth and Mary Habershon, John Goodwin, Lydia Mpanga Sebuyira, Andrew Kasirye, Joyce Mpanga, Rita Nkemba, Bishop Zac Niringiye, Adam Wood, Graham Carr, Patrick Shanahan, Jember Teferra, Danny and Rachel John, Patrick Macdonald, David Peppiatt, Andy Matheson, Sarah de Carvalho and 180 Alliance; and over forty deeply committed staff team members I was privileged to appoint and work alongside who served faithfully and sacrificially. As Retrak's President Emeritus it is a privilege to share recent exciting developments in the work led by David King (Chair), Diarmuid O Neill (CEO), Maggie Crewes, Dinah Mwesigye and teams in Ethiopia and Uganda. I acknowledge them and street child workers across the world. Thanks to hundreds of individuals, churches, trusts and groups who supported us over the years, to my dear parents and wider family and finally to every single street child I have been privileged to know and journey with.

Use of photographs

Cover pictures were taken with the permission and agreement of the subject, in accordance with relevant sections of Retrak's child protection policy at the time. We promoted the use of positive images in publicity and stipulated that children were offered copies of portrait photographs taken.

Names

Names of children whose stories are related in this book have been changed to protect their identity.

1 Introduction

While children go hungry, as they do now, I'll fight; while there is a poor lost girl upon the street . . . I'll fight – I'll fight to the very end.

General William Booth, founder of The Salvation Army, 1906. Quoted in J. Evan Smith, 1949

If we imagine working with street children as a fight, this book represents reports and reflections from the front, recommendations and kit for those in service, guidance for new recruits and principles for decision-makers. Our combat is against injustice and the abuse of power, deprivation and neglect, apathy and indifference. Street children, who we fight for, need to accompany us and to engage with the struggle in order to advance and for vision to become reality. The less militaristic metaphor and language of journeying with street children is at the heart of the approach explored. Before venturing ahead, let's consider who our travelling companions are.

Jehovah knew us for two years before he expressed an interest in returning home. He had lived on the street – or more accurately, in a street child 'depot' – for seven years and was used to fending for himself. A physically strong lad, Jehovah was influential amongst street boys and survived by growing food in a hidden corner of the golf course. He was arrested frequently and we first met him in the city remand home. He heard that his family needed assistance digging the land and after careful preparation, we visited the home with him. We discovered his father had suffered a stroke and was paralysed on one side of his body. It transpired that the family felt let down by Jehovah when he ran away at the age of 11. They had courageously protected him during the aftermath of civil war and needed to know he understood the sacrifices they had made before accepting him into the family again. Jehovah lay prostrate in front of his father and begged forgiveness. I will never forget the long silence as we awaited the reply. A pardon was granted and the family embraced. During the months that followed, Jehovah reintegrated into family and community life and cultivated the land.

Alfred was eight years old when the team found him begging on the street. He came to the centre and shortly afterwards took us to where he was living. He was the sole carer of an uncle with Down's syndrome. The floor of the tiny, dark room they shared was covered with rotten fruit peelings. Alfred's only other relative was his grandfather – the local drunk who had gone missing. With our support, a neighbour offered to accommodate Alfred and the local headmaster allowed him free schooling. Shortly afterwards he appeared at our clinic with a stomach abscess, exacerbated by poor diet, and was rushed into hospital. While convalescing after surgery, he told alarming stories of the neighbour's involvement in witchcraft practices. These were verified which heightened our awareness and taught us important lessons about assessment, risks and timing. Alfred was instead cared for in the halfway home before being fostered by a carefully selected carer. She provided support and security which enabled Alfred to thrive and progress academically, beyond all expectations.

These snapshots, from the lives of just two of many unique individuals we were privileged to journey with, illustrate the range and complexity of issues facing street children and in the case of Alfred, how multiple deprivations co-exist in the life of just one child. The approach explored in this book was a response to needs expressed by children such as Alfred and Jehovah. In order to depict it accurately, I have set parameters which establish what the aims of this book are.

This book is *not* a biographical or narrative account. It does, however, incorporate stories, anecdotes and references to our journey to emphasise key aspects of the approach described, to highlight issues to consider and to inspire and encourage readers.

This book does *not* even attempt to define 'street children' or give global statistics. You may be surprised and possibly relieved to read that. There are many books, articles and discussion papers reflecting unending debates about definitions, proposing up-to-date terminology and describing insurmountable difficulties of knowing how many street children there are. Some such publications and resources are given as references. This book does, however, emphasise the need for firstly *clarity* and secondly *perspective*.

- *Clarity* about who we are working with or intend to. Since setting out on this journey in 1995, street children have been classified as 'part-time', 'full-time', 'on', 'of' and 'in' the street and preferred labels currently include street-involved, street-dependent and street-connected. Efforts to define and categorise vary in their usefulness at grassroots level. What is crucial is to define who *you* intend to work with. The scale and scope of operations will depend on the nature and depth of response to those who fall within your definition. In order to achieve the objectives of lasting transformation and permanent alternatives to the street in the community, we defined the 'target group' we would prioritise as children and young people between the ages of 7 and 20 years old who spent both day and night on the street. We failed at times to review whether we were *still* reaching the intended target group or had unintentionally weakened our impact by ineffective gate keeping. This is discussed in detail in Chapter 3. In Uganda we worked specifically with boys because of tensions and differences between the street boy and street girl population which manifested in failed attempts to integrate. We identified the need for a separate or parallel programme to address specific and complex issues faced by girls and referred girls to organisations able to do so. We also offered technical support to those intending to develop work with street girls. In other contexts, where issues are less pronounced, mixed-gender programmes are appropriate and effective.
- *Perspective* and awareness based on accurate information. Although global statistics may be elusive, counting street children within each context is possible. We participated in an ambitious 'head-count' over a long period in 1997 spearheaded by a lead agency and this informed our planning and practice. For similar reasons, we hosted research students who mapped out the street child population and made significant conclusions about demographics and mobility. An awareness of numbers and trends in your city or region is vital to prioritise,

plan and review effectively and to maintain perspective on your work and its impact by placing it within a wider picture.

This book is *not* an academic tome but relates theory and insight to practice. Pioneering new work entailed action-centred learning, the outcomes of which are the basis of this book. A 'dream plan' articulated in 1997 was based on; an agreed vision, background experience, training and understanding of social work principles and processes; a commitment to contextual relevance; preparation and sensitivity to cross-cultural work. Aspects of the programme were imagined and designed, implemented and then reviewed. Some proved effective, others needed to be adapted or abandoned.

This book is *not* an overview of global initiatives with street children but by sharing experience and insight from one country during a specific period of time, it is a reference point which may encourage or aid critical self-reflection in any context. There are myriad references to the significance of cultural and contextual relevance and I am acutely aware from visits and reading that no two places or projects are the same. That is not to diminish the value of such reading and visits. I depended heavily on advice from and exposure to other practitioners even if it reinforced conviction about why we did things in certain ways or highlighted differences between their approach and ours. Judith Ennew is a prolific writer, widely respected among those working with street children and youth. She challenges assumptions made about street children being a homogenous group and urges critical examination of constructs of childhood itself. In regard to the 'African Child' and then to street children she states:

> It is difficult to see what, apart from geography, makes a Cairo shoeshine boy, a ten year old domestic servant in Lagos . . . and an Ethiopian youngster herding camels fall under the same rubric of the African Child . . . besides being influenced by adultist assumptions, research about children who live and work on the streets of urban Africa also has to contend with constructions of childhood that have little to do with African context.

Her global perspective enables her to issue a warning to those working in an African context:

> The imposition of a Latin American model of street children is bound to be fundamentally incorrect. In the first place it denies the differences that exist between Latin American contexts, which are mirrored in differences in street children's lives and activities.
>
> Ennew, 2003

Whilst endorsing Ennew's far-reaching conclusions, I still believe there is common ground and hope this book can influence practitioners in all parts of the world. A widely accepted element of best practice, in whatever setting, is reflective analysis and review. The organisation I led has adapted and refined some areas since I changed role. If that was not the case, it would contradict the viewpoint propounded – that we need to tune and re-tune into our context and environment.

Finally, this book does *not* offer a prescriptive methodology for working with street children.

Instead, it explores a tried and tested approach in order to draw out principles, some of which transcend culture, and their practical application in one context.

The approach is five-fold and summed up as:

- holistic
- relational
- transitional
- child-centred
- professional

These aspects are addressed separately in the following five chapters but must be treated as parts of a whole. Their meaning and significance are only understood in relation to each other, so readers need to reach the end of the book to fully grasp the approach. Key aspects became known as the 'five pillars' of our work and we used and referred to them to review work, assess impact and prioritise. To stretch the analogy, the five pillars are finely balanced. If one is removed, the building collapses – or is severely distorted. The approach is untenable or weakened if one element is missing or ignored.

Each chapter follows a similar pattern. Definitions and fundamental principles, which are foundational to thinking in the ways proposed, are considered. Terms and phrases are subject to deconstruction in an attempt to add weight and meaning to our language and enable clear articulation of what we do and why. Once the necessary groundwork has been done, practical applications are considered. Experiences and lessons from both disappointments and achievements are shared.

This introduction is followed by Chapter 2, which explores holistic thinking. It covers key areas of understanding children, designing a programme, forming and building a team, leadership and networking. Some of Retrak's history and background is outlined to illustrate programme design. A relational approach is considered in Chapter 3 and after discussing implications for the culture and leadership of an organisation, relationship-based social work is highlighted as intrinsic to such an approach. The practical application of a relational approach is divided into six key elements; entering the world of street children, engaging with street children, forming authentic relationship, hearing and listening, recognising and responding to trauma and assessment which entails constructing and testing hypotheses. An understanding of transference is essential in relational work. It is introduced before moving to the next pillar.

Chapter 4, the longest by far, discusses the meaning and implementation of a transitional approach which emanates from valuing and understanding family and community. An unavoidable discussion about institutional care ensues before looking in detail, in five appendices, at elements of a transitional approach; drop in centres, transitional education, residential care, reconciliation and reunification with relatives, integration into existing families (foster care). In each case the purposes are related to an overarching vision and key issues and questions are identified.

Chapters 5 and 6 consider what it means in theory and in practice to be child-centred and professional – the final two pillars of the approach explored. The themes of childhood and development, participation, empowerment and choice underpin child-centred practice and manifest in counselling methods, measuring impact, child forums and leadership. Thinking professionally entails being selective, strategic and focussed, establishing values, principles and ethics and a commitment to personal development and responsibility. Two major aspects of a professional approach — developing core social work competencies and human resource development — are introduced.

The story of how work began in Uganda is scattered throughout the book but Chapter 7 summarises the process prior to a work being launched in Ethiopia. Intentionally, getting started is left until this chapter, as readers considering new initiatives with street children will have a deeper understanding of what one approach entails. Increased awareness will hopefully lead to improved and more realistic planning.

Chapter 8 is inevitably short, as it skims the surface and begs further discussion about significant aspects of working with street children; advocacy, prevention and funding, and Chapter 9 offers both challenge and encouragement to those working with or on behalf of street children.

At a staff team retreat we imagined our work as a tree and what the roots, branches and fruit may signify. It was a worthwhile and poignant exercise and enabled us to step back from the everyday hassles and processes that are represented in the pages of this book. I would urge planners and practitioners alike to similarly reflect, imagine, review and dream.

Our **vision** was of a world where no child had to live on the street.

Our **mission** was to enable children to realise their potential and discover their worthwhile offering permanent alternatives to the street. The children we empowered did not belong to us. They were not 'our boys'. When a city council asked me to assess how a split in the leadership of a children's home had affected residents, I discovered that possessive attitudes and language used by leaders compounded the children's experience of trauma. To deter such thinking we banned possessive language in meetings and avoided it in publicity. Instead, we nurtured and communicated the idea of journeying with street children.

Our **business** was rebuilding lives, restoring dignity and releasing potential. To do so we had to resist the 'ah-but-it'll-never-work-here syndrome', embark on a journey and develop an **approach** that I now feel privileged to share with you.

2 A Holistic Approach

Introduction

Defining a holistic approach

There is a lot of talk about approaching and doing things holistically but what does it mean? Holistic haircuts, holistic holidays in Greece, holistic insurance policies, dog food, massage and resorts, holistic marketing and advertising, holistic agriculture and horse riding are all on offer. 'Holistic' has been a buzz word in medicine and alternative therapies for a long time, in education more recently and many street child networks and organisations now refer in their literature to a 'holistic approach'. It's out there as an impressive catchphrase which evokes a favourable response from public and donors but two huge questions spring to mind; firstly, 'what does it actually *mean*?' And secondly, 'how is it demonstrated in our planning and practical working with street children?'

'Holism' has only been in existence as a word for the past century – since 1926 according to one source – and refers to acknowledging things in their entirety. Dictionary definitions suggest holism is a philosophical theory that a system is greater than the sum of its parts or that life is made up of organic or unified wholes that are greater than the sum of their parts. A holistic approach looks at the whole picture. It assumes that a situation or system cannot be fully understood by breaking it down into component parts and examining them in isolation.

Defining a holistic approach within social work

Before considering what a holistic approach looks like in practice, we need to clarify exactly what it means in a social work context. The International Federation of Social Workers describes social work broadly in the following way:

> Social work in its various forms addresses the multiple, complex transactions between people and their environments. Its mission is to enable people to develop their full potential, enrich their lives and prevent dysfunction . . . The holistic focus of social work is universal, but the priorities of social work practice will vary from country to country and from time to time depending on cultural, historical, and socio-economic conditions.
>
> IFSW Review, 2010

Holistic social work organisations and workers demonstrate awareness of the entire situation surrounding individuals they are entrusted to work with. No single organisation or worker can possibly respond to every aspect of a person's life but every organisation and worker that claims to be holistic must:

- Receive and assimilate lots of information from a wide range of sources.
- Reflect on how parts of an individual's life inter-relate to each other.
- Accept perspectives and information that may shed new light and challenge previous conclusions reached.

The last of these three processes *will* demand open-mindedness and humility initially and *may* demand flexibility and creativity later on in shaping or reshaping our response. If you are or could be involved in developing a team working in a holistic way, these abilities and qualities should be prioritised in recruiting workers and in training and development to nurture growth in these areas. The application of a holistic approach relates not only to social workers, key workers and counsellors but also to staff members from other disciplines or professional background and to leaders.

If they are expected to work together in a holistic way, every member of the team needs to demonstrate aptitude for and commitment to develop open mindedness, humility, flexibility and creativity.

So a holistic approach within social work seeks to understand an individual person as a unique and whole being, more than the sum of his or her parts and existing within a context or environment. It affects the way teams operate and members relate. It should be reflected in who we recruit, the internal dynamics of an organisation and the way it relates to and with peer organisations. It determines priorities and sets an agenda for all social and key workers to be agents of change in individual lives, families, communities and society.

Holistic thinking

We've attempted to define a holistic approach within social work but to really grasp its meaning and to ensure it impacts and inspires our practice it must underpin and determine our understanding of personhood.

Key concept of the person as an integrated whole

Component parts of a person may include; health, physical attributes, appearance, childhood experience, mental and emotional state, self esteem, trauma, educational ability, talents, family structure and dynamics, sibling order and relationships, culture, social and political context, economic status, spirituality and faith, aspirations and expectations. These and other component parts are all significant and could be treated in isolation from each other. Holistic thinking, however, gives significance to their inter-relationship – the way they mesh together to produce a unique individual. It impacts how we view and understand each person as an integrated whole. It stirs us to acknowledge a person's intrinsic potential and worth.

To think and act holistically the street child worker needs to understand each street child as a unique individual within a wider context. Starting or developing that process might involve exploring the inter-connectedness of different aspects of who we are. The following are examples or illustrations of thinking holistically about ourselves:

The relationship between self-esteem and health

Self-esteem is discussed in depth elsewhere. For now, consider how we feel about or value ourselves when we are sick. The physical condition permeates our thinking and beliefs about ourselves. Conversely, consider our emotional state or sense of worth when we are physically well and vibrant. One aspect leads to another so physical exercise can lead to better and deeper sleep which for some enables a calmer response to possible threats to our self esteem and so on. Considering possible cycles of cause and effect and the interplay between us and our circumstances are examples of holistic thinking.

The relationship between social groups, relating to others and self-perception

Imagine how you behave and react when surrounded by different groups of people – by those with similar academic achievements to you, by those with much higher achievements and finally by those with significantly lower achievements. Your surrounding can shape how you feel about yourself – and that affects your behaviour in a group setting, confidence, decision-making and ability to befriend. Social setting, self-esteem, confidence, behaviour and relationships may be linked in a cyclical process which perpetuates itself. Identifying those links is a way of viewing behaviour holistically.

How sibling order or rivalry may impact other aspects of who we are

For the author movement classes during training for the acting profession were challenging not least because of what they revealed about each of us! Social work and acting overlap in the realm of empathy. The purpose of empathising may differ but the common ground is grasping what makes a person who they are and seeing the world through their eyes, walking in their shoes or more aptly in the case of street children feeling the ground with their bare feet. That means considering them holistically. This was demonstrated in classes considering our physicality and in particular how we walk. After several attempts we were able to walk in front of a group of fellow actors in a neutral and natural way. The surprise came when my movement teacher said 'From what I've seen and learned, I would guess you are the youngest member of your family'. He was unnervingly right. Something about the way I carried myself across the hall combined with his observations and understanding of me to that point, indicated something about how I perceived myself from which he formed a hypothesis about where that perception may have come from. He was thinking holistically about sibling rivalry, self-awareness and esteem, movement and physicality.

Empathy is not self indulgent because for both actor and social or youth worker, it is a means to an end. It is a core tool, a skill and a discipline to be developed. Reflecting on self helps us to develop empathy with those we portray on stage or screen or those we are privileged to work amongst. If empathy is the 'means', then truthful performance for an actor and improved lives of street children for social or key workers are the 'ends' we seek.

Understanding personality in a holistic way

For practitioners, team leaders and managers alike, an understanding of personhood, personality and how we relate to the world around us are foundational to a holistic approach to working with street children. There are many tools that can be used to build awareness of and explore personality. I enthuse about the Myers-Briggs Type Indicator (MBTI©) and the huge amount of work that stems from it. In a nutshell, the MBTI is based on four opposite pairs of preferences (or 'dichotomies') which describe how people see the world, receive and process information and how they make decisions. Rather than reducing us to one of sixteen personality 'types' it opens a whole world of possibilities and meanings once we identify our four preferences and understand how they impact each other. The MBTI is a holistic tool. It views personality itself as more than the sum of its parts. You may be an 'extrovert' (E) but the meaning or application of that alters slightly according to which of the other preferences or temperaments you fall in to. It's the grouping, the unique combination or the whole that counts and that's what makes it holistic. Few people land on exactly the same point on all four spectrums between opposite preferences. Individuals respond differently to stress, some leaning even more heavily toward their preference while others retreat toward the opposite preference. Rather than reducing an individual to a personality clone, this tool and others like it deepen and expand our vision and understanding.

It's a living tool evolving all the time and I recommend it to help build team and community so long as it is taken with the *seriousness* it deserves and under the *supervision* that it requires.

David Keirsey's academic work (1984), which led to the reframing of the Myers Briggs personality types into a system of four *temperaments*, was preceded by 20 years of working with young people – many of them in trouble with the law and from extremely difficult backgrounds. He caused controversy in some areas but his work is fascinating for a deeper understanding of human nature and behaviour. He demonstrates how temperaments vary in the following areas – interests, strengths, orientation, values, self-image and social roles. This book is about working with street children and that entails understanding each individual child – what they enjoy (interests) and what they are good at (strengths), what drives or leads them (orientation), what they hold dear (values), how they see themselves (self image) and what part do they or could they play in the community (social roles). The tools mentioned also increased our understanding of colleagues and team members. To build an effective team we need to gain a wider and deeper understanding of the whole person. To do so is to think and then act holistically.

Thinking holistically about poverty and difficult circumstances

The next stage on our exploration of a holistic approach is to consider what it means in relation to needs and difficult circumstances. It means refusing to reduce a child's situation to one cause or even a much quoted list of causes. It means placing individuals and their needs in context and hypothesising on the interplay of factors many of which were mentioned in the last paragraph.

Many writers have analysed poverty and its' meaning. Matheson relates marginalisation and ostracism to poverty and encourages us to consider types and dimensions of it:

> Poverty has many guises. While the immediate face of poverty is often economic, that is seldom the key issue . . . The destitute poor don't live in community. They live fragmented lives dictated by fragmented thoughts . . . For the working poor, it is often the lack of choice that is the debilitating factor.
>
> Matheson, 2010

Paul Collier's *The Bottom Billion* (2008) is described as extraordinarily important. He considers poverty holistically by linking it to four traps – conflict, lack of natural resources, being landlocked and bad governance, and writes, 'Poverty is not intrinsically a trap, otherwise we would all still be poor.

National and international conferences on the issue of street children I attend invariably feature at least one presenter declaring, 'The main cause of street children is poverty.' This is increasingly frustrating as it reduces a complex set of circumstances and responses to them to a single word. In fact I would go further and say that such non-holistic thinking or lack of serious thought does a disservice to the number of families who, despite abject poverty, do not abandon or marginalise children to the extent that they leave home. Of course poverty can have the effect of magnifying issues and limiting problem-solving possibilities so the critical question for those thinking holistically should be:

> What was the tipping point that made marginalisation or abandonment of children a seemingly acceptable outcome within the life of a family, community or even society?

The answers will be as numerous and as complex as the street children you work or will work with. They will be found by thinking holistically in the way that has been outlined and that is essential before considering what a holistic approach means in practice.

Holistic practice

Engaging children as more than the sum of their parts

Practical implications of working in a holistic way are discussed in detail in other chapters. They include the following:

- Developing a 360° view of each child which informs the content and technique of counselling.
- Understanding and handling challenging behaviour by placing it in context.
- Enabling street children to make decisions and understand themselves and future possibilities.
- Increasing choices and offering guidance in an appropriate way.

- Avoiding forming opinions and conclusions too early and being willing to test hypotheses against other perspectives.
- Resisting compartmentalising technical knowledge and expertise, being flexible and willing to change.
- Acknowledging the impact of environment, social and political landscape.
- Ensuring the programme serves the individual and not the other way round.

One reality of working with street children is that they are like any other children. That means that at times they have the ability to drive you up the wall and can trigger responses you had not realised you were capable of. If working with street children seems a breeze, I would question whether you are reaching the right target group and if you are, whether they are yet able to express and be themselves fully.

First impressions rarely reveal a true or complete picture. Visitors are highly esteemed in most African contexts and great efforts are made to welcome and impress. That fact, combined with the tendency of children who have lacked secure attachment to clamber for attention and affection, means that visitors to street child agencies have a positive, heart warming encounter but rarely see the full picture. In Uganda, where a 'pedestal mentality' sometimes exists toward visitors from Europe or the States, even short-term volunteers may leave with an incomplete view of the children they came to serve. That's one reason we preferred volunteers to come for at least two years with humility and willingness to learn rather than a desire to 'change the world' or become a 'hero' to children. Street children can be extremely challenging to work with. Yet at times they were extraordinarily strong, inventive, fun, gifted and resilient such as Godfrey who wrote:

> I was being harassed by my mother so I escaped to Kampala in 1998 where I joined my elder brother. Every morning I would walk to Owino market to carry luggage for shoppers. I parted from my brother when he stole money from my labour and ended up in a 'depot' called kakuta. I slept there for almost a year before Tigers Club took me in as a patient at the refuge. My hardest time came when I discovered I had cancer and had to part with one of my legs. I thought I would never be myself again but because of the love and sympathy given to me by the boys and staff I have got more confidence and thank everyone who has shown me love.

One Christmas Eve I sat with Godfrey following the amputation of his leg. Even after extensive chemotherapy to fight the remaining cancer, he impressed the hospital staff with his spirit and determination. At the Clubhouse he helped with the clinic and became known as 'omusawo' (doctor). When a visitor arrived he would be the first to the gate to offer a huge smile and welcome. He was fitted with a prosthetic leg and given a three-wheel bike to enable him to live independently but 18 months later cancer appeared on his lung. With the help of Hospice Uganda we relieved his pain and ensured that when the struggle was finally over he died with dignity. Visitors wrote to say how Godfrey's smile and spirit had affected theirs. One person went further and said, 'Godfrey taught me what it meant to be human'.

Responding to Godfrey in a holistic way meant placing his immediate needs in context, enabling him to thrive despite obvious challenges, celebrating his strengths and personality and ultimately prioritising his dignity and quality of relationships and life right to the end. In summary, it entailed engaging with Godfrey holistically – as someone who was more than the sum of his parts.

Designing a programme more than the sum of its activities

It is misleading to assume that all organisations or projects working holistically with street children look the same or to suggest that each project must meet the diverse needs of every child. A truly holistic organisation *will not* operate in isolation from other organisations or the wider community. It will not attempt to offer a 'solution' that ignores the need for other perspectives and services. It acknowledges other aspects of a child's life even if they are not yet fully known or revealed. Sadly, many organisations do operate in isolation and claim to be a one-stop solution. They may come across as superior and some, in my experience, have other agendas they are seeking to fulfil.

A truly holistic street child organisation *will* start with the person at the centre and work outwards. It means designing a programme but placing it within the wider political, social and cultural context and alongside other organisations and the services they provide. It means relating what you are doing to the outside world in a way that reflects our understanding of what it means to be a whole person, our deeper exploration of personality and our awareness that background and environment are not just significant in the life of a child but *intrinsically* part of the life of that child or young person.

The *Retrak* programme we developed in Uganda is an example of one that aimed to be holistic. Like so many charities and NGOs, it began as a 'hobby charity' that sought to build bridges with the growing community of street boys in the capital Kampala and to discover more about their backgrounds and needs. It used sport under the banner of Tigers Football Club to engage with a particular group of lads and within a short period of time word spread and around 200 were turning up for training and then matches. The founders of Tigers FC quickly recognised that physical needs had to be met before or alongside the needs for recreation and belonging which the club provided. So began the feeding programme and provision of basic medical services through a volunteer nurse and team of assistants trained in first aid.

As street children realised what was on offer and that the founders were genuine in their intent, they became more relaxed and able to be themselves. That led them to disclose real needs and bring learned behaviour to the pitch so incidence of fighting and verbal abuse increased and demands for attention grew. Those were encouraging indications that the right target group were being reached. Over time an environment would be created that offered alternatives to resolving conflict violently which is something we will come back to. Ambience does not develop over night – it took several years before fights, drug misuse and verbal attacks at the pitch-side and drop in centre reduced significantly. Even then it was healthy for kids to feel safe enough to be real and occasional disruption – through aggression, stealing or shouting – to that sought after ambience, served as salient reminders of the world of street children and confirmed we were drawing the right target group and not simply attracting children from the neighbouring slums.

Prior to addressing some of the wider needs of boys at the football club, foundations of a holistic approach were laid by recognising the inter-connection between physical needs for nutrition, health and recreation and the psychological needs for belonging, acceptance and stability. More than that, attention was given to the wider social challenges faced by the lads. Links were made between their behaviour and abuse encountered on the street, from older street boys or by police and security guards and experience in cells, courts and remand homes. Before we arrived in Uganda in 1996, these aspects of many boys' daily lives were being addressed. Through appearances in court, visits to remand homes, resolving conflict within or between the 'depots' where groups of street children lived, the team were responding in a holistic way.

It resonated with what I had experienced and learned in residential work with former heroin addicts in Scotland. What struck me with force was that compartmentalising a young person's life did nothing to serve either that young person's deep need or to protect the wider community. I encountered survival crime in a way I hadn't before and am grateful to the residents for teaching me so much about the associated nature and power of craving. Although my attempts to use drama were met with a steely eyed response and strong language, the art and literary work was more successful. Powerful painting and rich poetry drove home that an addict's relationship with their heroin is with a 'lover'. I vividly recall how, in court, residents' offending behaviour was discussed with little, if any, reference to cause and effect, to the wider context of social pressure and survival crime or to the inner turmoil expressed through their art and poetry. In court and the issuing of harsh words and stiff sentences, they counted for nothing.

Two years after the launch of Tigers FC, we had to establish what our main activities were and acknowledge our strengths and limitations. To formally register as an NGO we had to think this through carefully but more importantly for the sake of those we were seeking to help and for like-minded peer organisations with whom we might partner and collaborate in a meaningful way. There was tension for a while between us and some more established groups – the founders of which made grandiose claims about knowing every single street child in Kampala and claiming to be the answer rather than seeking to work together. On one occasion we were challenged to be the organisation that 'did sport' and leave other aspects of a child's needs to other groups. The idea was that together we would be holistic – one providing education, another food, another medical services, another vocational training and Tigers Club providing sport because 'that is what you are good at and what you know'.

I understood the point but knew there were risks around responsibility and children drifting, that motives had to be checked and transparent and that a balance was needed to avoid on one hand the compartmentalising referred to above and on the other becoming an organisation that claimed to be all things to all children. The balance came when we recognised what we could do well and what we couldn't. Our scope would allow us to be an effective social work organisation which could reach young people through football, meet some fundamental welfare needs, provide appropriate education and agricultural training to street children who had missed school or participation in digging the land, address deeper psycho-social needs through counselling and reconcile children with families, integrate others into foster families or assist them to become independent. These aspects and how they inter-relate are shown in the diagram illustrating The Tigers Club original programme. What we **could not** provide was formal education in line with mainstream curricula or more than basic medical services or vocational skills training. Those things would have to be provided for through other agencies and partner organisations.

We became an organisation with a clearly defined and fairly narrow target group rather than attempting to meet the needs of a broad base of children in difficult circumstances. We focussed on a relationship-based approach that would lead to lasting change. In other words we aimed to go deeper with fewer for as long as it would take. Therefore, rather than create another vocational training college, which would have attracted donors, we formed strong links with colleges that offered a range of courses. Retrak fulfilled its' unique parental role. One principal said that his college's original aim was to serve street children but it could only do so with a support organisation – not just to assist with fees but to ensure wider needs were being met and there was a point of contact with the outside world that could create stability, address issues as they arose and give extra support to those who have known life on the street. Synergy was created by two or more organisations responding to an individual's needs in a holistic way. Both aimed to 'be holistic' in their approach but neither tried to be provide everything for every child.

The diagram below summarises much of what has been said and shows a possible pathway from the street, through the programme and into the community. Children rarely went through in a regular or uniform way but the diagram was a useful tool to explain the programme. Many parts are described later and referring back to the chart should add clarity.

We have considered what a programme that seeks to be holistic might and might not feature. The illustration given is an organisation which comprises of many parts but recognises it cannot be all things to all children so defines its target group and purpose, identifies its strengths and limitations and finds peer organisations with which to partner in order to fulfil their common desire to 'be holistic'. Those are the ingredients but in practise how do we ensure the component parts complement each other and reflect the understanding of each child being greater than the sum of their parts? To extend the cooking analogy, how do we put the ingredients together to create a cake that will rise to its full potential?

The Baraza Principle

One answer I believe to be applicable in all settings and cultures is found in what I call the 'baraza principle'. *Baraza* is a Swahili word that literally means the veranda outside a home but is also used to refer to what happens on the veranda. It's a place for gathering and lively discussion, a place for village elders and residents to bring their different views on a problem or issue in order to come up with a communal solution. That is the essence of the gatherings I am talking about – a coming together of people with different perspectives to share and discuss, plan and review. I carried out 184 resettlements of street children and on initial and follow up visits a 'baraza' would sometimes happen spontaneously around the event of the child's return

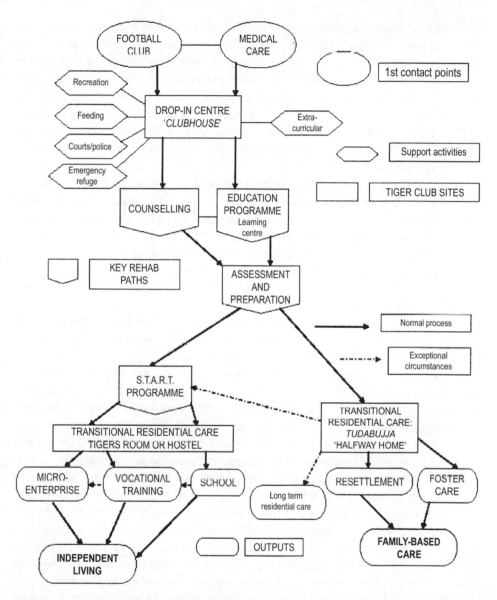

Diagram used to explain the original Tigers Club programme

or specific challenges being faced. The local chairman (LC1) a teacher, neighbours, relatives and church leaders may be among those present.

At the Tigers Club, the weekly meeting for all staff was when individuals were discussed and anything pertinent noted. As the organisation grew, it became necessary for a separate meeting which focussed solely on individuals so we decided a case conference or 'baraza' should be held monthly or every six weeks. We readily called these gatherings 'case conferences' until an international donor agency suggested they were an example of western social work practice being imposed in an African situation! In fact nothing could have been further from the truth – there is nothing culturally exclusive about coming together in this way and it was a Ugandan colleague who first described our meetings as barazas. In the UK, unless such multi-disciplinary meetings relate to child protection, they are now called review or care planning meetings rather than case conferences. The name is less important than the principle behind it and whether it is put into practice.

The length of each baraza was between three and four hours, chaired by the director or head of social work. They were attended by social workers and project workers allocated to specific children, residential care workers and other staff when called upon. A simple format was followed of reviewing specific children from previous meetings and then going systematically through different departments firstly focussing on those already on the programme, then on new arrivals and finally potential cases. The number of cases discussed in depth was usually around 25. The average length of time allocated to each child was around nine minutes although some inevitably took much longer than others.

Team members were asked to share information and insights so that quality decisions could be made by the relevant worker. This openness and sense of joint responsibility were core elements of our work and when the system worked well the team felt listened to, supported and accountable to each other. In fact I would go further and say that what went on in those meetings touched the very nerve centre of the organisation in three ways; they reminded us of our purpose, enabled us to reflect on how we were doing individually and collectively and either reassured us that we were, or challenged us that we weren't, reaching the right target group. That third purpose was especially important for barazas which focussed on children at the drop in centre. Reaching the right target group depends firstly on effective 'gate-keeping' through aspects of the programme assigned this role. It also depends on gathering accurate and comprehensive information with children who come through the gates of a project to verify whether they match agreed criteria for further involvement. By way of contrast, the meetings or barazas at the halfway home focussed on children we already knew fitted those criteria. The majority could not be considered for resettlement with their families and so were being prepared for foster care. By implication these were individuals within a group for whom Tigers Club really existed in the first place – whose birth families could not or would not take responsibility for them. Even though the stories were tragic, I would return energised from these particular barazas as they went to the very heart of what we were doing.

It wasn't easy and we didn't always get it right. We should have been serious about implementing this plan earlier and diligent about ensuring they happened every six weeks irrespective of other demands upon us. If the gap between meetings was too long, the list of individual lads to be discussed became ridiculously long. Another reality was that meetings would end up focussing solely on the boys who were proving most challenging to understand, work with or see tangible signs of change. At times we recognised how this affected and distorted our thinking and perspective so included those who had fallen off our radar screens (because everything was basically going to plan) as a reminder that, at least for some, we were on target. Sometimes we slipped into a tick box mentality and lacked energy for creative thinking. The coordinator has a critical role to maintain balance and guide the process. They need to believe utterly in the value of such joint meetings, take ownership of them and motivate all staff to come ready to give and to receive.

When barazas went according to plan and were carefully recorded, we could track how individuals were responding to opportunities being created. Action plans were included in these records showing which staff team member would be doing what and when. As the minutes were available for all staff members including those not at the meetings, there was a growing awareness of who was doing what or who *should* have been doing what, to ensure consistency. They weren't always read of course but I remember drawing team members' attention to them especially if they interacted with the boys on a daily basis. One committed and energetic administrator started to respond harshly to one lad's verbal outbursts. She made some fairly stark conclusions about the reasoning behind his behaviour – until she was encouraged to read the findings and plans contained in the minutes of the baraza. Concurrently, what she experienced was noted and fed back to add to the key workers overall understanding of the child. Making notes available to staff teams assumes they have been trained to handle information in a sensitive way and honour the need for confidentiality.

So the 'Baraza Principle' is to enable individuals to work together in order to form stronger decisions and plans. Each aspect of a child's growth, development, background, personality and context should be represented and each worker involved with the child heard. The child himself or herself must be heard either directly or his wishes and desires accurately and faithfully represented. Every organisation is different and has to find what is right for its context and purpose but there is value in knowing what others do to spark new ideas, consolidate or question what's already being done. The following notes are from one meeting held at the halfway home, which illustrate different staff members' involvement and perspectives.

Richard – G (teacher) noted that Richard takes a long time to grasp and understand anything. This frustration may explain history of fighting at clubhouse as reported by C (warden). He has never been to school and was in Learning Centre prior to coming to Tudabujja. He found it hard to catch up so got demoralised and this led to absenteeism. T (residential care worker, [RCW]) shared that Richard needs continual affirmation and assurance as he fears being laughed at. After lessons he runs back to his cottage to check he has got something right. He enjoys making things and dismantling and rebuilding radios. It is intricate work which he seems to be skilled at.

S (senior social worker) reported that the resettlement visit to Kiyindi (via Lugazi) on Lake Victoria islands had failed (father had moved to another island) so Richard now says he only wants foster care. He has shared with RCWs that his father was once imprisoned for abusing him and that there were no other relatives. This was consistent with findings during counselling with D (foster care social worker). The meeting agreed that Richard should begin preparation for IFCS (foster care placement) and there should be further assessment of his learning difficulties.

Joshua – It was agreed that the previous occurrence of theft (July) would be dealt with by S (senior social worker) in the context of counselling/life story work as it seems to relate to so many other things that have been happening in Joshua's life.

Since then he ran away and returned, following discipline for rudeness to staff, (residential and teaching). Met with D (foster care social worker) yesterday who sensed a desire to conform and regret about repeatedly running away (effects explained diagrammatically). T (RCW) agreed and reported a reduction in crying but that issues remain about washing and grumbling, both of which are being addressed. He refuses to cooperate and frequently questions why he is asked to do things. A system of 'Daily Report' has been introduced and if he has clear report for 7 (then 14 & 28) consecutive days he will be rewarded.

A wider discussion was held in which team members suggested that his self-esteem seems low. Joshua believes and has complained of 'spirits' that are angry with him and T suggested that counselling and prayer, if asked for, may be needed. D remains uncertain that he is ready for foster care and that finding suitable carers will be a challenge and he will need additional support.

The notes above are simple and imperfect but serve to illustrate how different perspectives were considered. Whole staff meetings either side of the baraza meetings were opportunities to share with and hear from other team members. The following are necessary to get as comprehensive and accurate a picture as possible:

- Access and opportunity for comment from all team members, the children themselves and their peers.
- Information from both formal counselling and informal interaction (often with residential staff).
- Understanding of regional or cultural issues and expectations.
- Social work perspective and hypotheses formed.
- Development and attachment related issues and personality.
- Medical information.
- History and understanding of family.
- Impact of living on the street.
- Reports from educational and other activities about levels reached, behaviour, integration and others.
- Peer interaction and report from friends, older lads ('baabas' – mentors).

Building a team is more than the sum of its people

The programme described could only be implemented with a multi-disciplinary team of people who brought skills and commitment needed to work in a holistic way. The team grew over a nine year period from four to 22 full time staff members, which included trained social workers with different areas of expertise, teachers, administrators, a warden, project nurse, residential care workers, sports instructor, a farm manager/trainer, stores and operations managers, accountant and a director. In addition there were part time staff and volunteers on the feeding and medical programmes and security guards. At recruitment stage we were concerned with what in management parlance is referred to as 'organisational fit'. For us that meant showing aptitude for teamwork. Working in a holistic way impacts how we position our own role and work and how we view and relate to others. Although it is great to see specific teams within the wider team strengthened in identity and effectiveness, it should never be at the expense of working holistically.

The diagram on page 15 refers to four Tigers Club sites – the drop-in centre, the hostel (for boys in full-time education or vocational training) Tigers rooms (for those in vocational training or setting up small businesses) and the halfway home which is described in Chapter 4. The need for joined-up or holistic thinking was greater than if we had been in one location and the risk of teams within the larger team becoming possessive and thinking departmentally were higher. Attention and effort was needed to ensure that individuals firstly understood and then celebrated what others were doing, how it related to what they did and to the overall vision. We learned that communicating and demonstrating this should be a priority in the induction of new staff and learning the art of it a focus of staff team development. In other words, don't expect it to happen magically or overnight.

We were privileged to have on our team a football coach who had played for the national side, the Uganda Cranes. Steven was with us for seven years and his understanding of how football and sports under his leadership related to other parts of the programme grew organically as the project grew. We took this understanding for granted. Our failure to properly impart the overall vision to future coaches was a failing on our part and something we had to address by developing better induction for new members. The team itself is more than the sum of its parts but learning what that means takes time and effort.

Members of a team working in a holistic way need to:

- Recognise and develop their own expertise.
- Learn the art of understanding and appreciating others' work.
- Relate what they have found or learned to what others have found.

One word to sum this up is *complementarity* and is an essential ingredient of a holistic approach. Every member of the team needs to demonstrate commitment to complementarity. For teams of people with a range of professions to be effective, Sousa and Costa suggest that individuals must replace power and certainty (which flow from technical or specialist knowledge) with *curiosity* (which does not negate technical or specialist knowledge) and *empowerment* (which enables others). They suggest that workers need to be reflective and flexible in response to information shared rather than being 'reactive' which is an automatic response based solely on one's own knowledge.

Meetings and processes that facilitate complementarity within a team need to be well planned and coordinated. If they are not, individual children may drift through the programme. If all staff members feel they should be involved to some extent in a child's journey, it could mean that the child does not get the continuity and dedicated attention from specified individuals that he or she needs. Leaders need to ensure information is shared and accessible and to pay attention to possible division or rivalry.

Five years after registering in Uganda we opened the halfway home (Tudabujja). We were still pioneering new parts of the programme and there was a lot of excitement and creative energy around. Before any residents or staff had moved in we were aware that some team members were assuming the halfway home would become the focus of all operations and that the city centre base would become periphery. The dangers of thinking compartmentally rather than holistically were already being flagged up. There needed to be an understanding that each centre served the needs of the other. If there was to be a 'hub' we resolved it should be where the project came into contact with children still living on the street and that our response should be to what was happening right outside the gates of the Clubhouse. Tudabujja would evolve as a centre of healing and restoration in preparation for life in the community but it had to depend heavily on the team at the Clubhouse to both identify and prepare the right children with the right focus and understanding to enter at the right time. Regular and good quality communications, visits, joint meetings were all put in place to ensure mutual understanding and respect. When we as leaders failed to protect these areas, suspicion and power struggles emerged and temporarily derailed the process of working in a holistic way:

> *The multi-professional approach can be described as a process for reaching goals that cannot be achieved by working alone. It is a process whereby parties who see different aspects of a problem can explore their differences and search for solutions beyond their own vision of what is possible.*
>
> Sousa and Costa, 2010

What an inspiring thought that as street child workers work together in a holistic way we will find solutions for street children beyond our own vision of what we think is possible! So investing time to develop a team was not for introspective reasons but to strengthen work and deepen impact with street children we were privileged to work with. Team development is in my view not an optional add-on but an ethical responsibility of any social work organisation. In the UK there are compulsory minimum contact hours set for social workers to spend with supervisors. Supervision may vary in quality but the point here is that support and development should be inherent in work with children and young people facing difficult circumstances. I have witnessed and experienced the effects of burnout. The energetic worker becomes numb to the purpose in front of him and her. It is debilitating and demoralising and has a ripple effect on even the strongest of teams. Managers or Board members should note that burnout is preventable and that the risk of occurrence can be managed and minimised. Don't short change frontline staff in the area of personal and team development and support. They are essentials, not luxuries. In practise we committed to three staff team development days a year and one staff team residential retreat. As the team grew so did the costs in terms of finance and workload increase but the need was just as great.

The purpose of such times was *to create a safe environment for a team to grow and develop.* It is worthwhile making parallels with family life. Staff and leaders of street child organisations have a duty to be a model to children deprived of a functioning and healthy family. Communication and respect are core to building levels of trust needed for family life to thrive. Team Development Days would address these and other issues. We discovered that the order had to be changed – respect first and then communication. Even with protocols and procedures in place and multiple methods of communication available, if there was no respect, communication didn't flow. There had to be a common understanding of each others' roles and responsibilities, respect for them and a desire to communicate to make any structures and systems put in place have any impact. With new members coming on board and the risk of long serving members of staff becoming complacent, we had to constantly reflect and review but staff team days and retreats were good opportunities to focus on how we were doing.

Examples of themes explored during team development days and retreats

Roles and responsibilities

As the team grew the need to clarify roles and responsibilities seemed to grow even faster! Each addition to the team resulted in a more complex web of relationships and it was not enough to send a memo or write on a board what someone's role was. Mutual respect only emerged when trust developed within the team. Trust only surfaced with understanding and effective communication between us all. Development days included finding innovative ways of developing these aspects of team life. Without occasional hard discussions, misunderstanding and unspoken pressures will remain and in time manifest in less positive ways.

Empathy exercises and role play

There was something very powerful about doing this as a multi-disciplinary team. Different perspectives and insights are shared to strengthen our mutual understanding of the world of a street child. Empathy should be taken seriously and may be hard as we feel others pain but in this context there was scope for laughter and creativity. Hot-seating staff acting out being a street child meant quizzing them in ways you may not in reality. Responses were accepted but maybe challenged later to really get under the skin of the character being portrayed.

Resolving conflict together

The emphasis was on a collaborative response to challenging or potentially dangerous behaviour. Fights which broke out on a regular basis indicated that we were reaching the right target group. On one morning four staff members were involved breaking up an incident. Two of us retrieved six knives and ended up with spectacularly blood soaked shirts. We needed an opportunity to offload after such occasions and even more so after experiences where one or two lads had threatened or abused an individual staff member. A good supervisor or line manager will offer support to an individual but the team day was a chance to analyse in a safe environment what had happened and how we could improve practice in resolving conflict. We explored tactics and timing, language and non-verbal communication and recognising when and how to back up fellow staff members. The issue of conflict resolution is discussed in detail in the section on running a drop in centre in Chapter 4.

In depth review of specific individuals

Frontline workers explored in pairs one child who had responded in a positive way and one who had not. The first was the individual they were most likely to tell others about with excitement and even joy. The second would be the one who they had found most draining and maybe even tried to avoid.

There were several light-bulb moments during team development days which shed light on our work and highlighted their importance.

Creating a network more than the sum of its NGOs

Agali awamu ge galuma ennyama
Teeth with no gaps, is what bites the meat

For several years at the drop in centre, I had an office which I shared with another social worker and which also served as a counselling and meeting room. It was likened to Piccadilly Circus at rush hour. There were cooking and washing areas right outside its window and the stream of requests, phone calls, arguments going on outside, staffing issues and general noise made it challenging at times. However it was good to be at the heart of things rather than in an isolated place and the arrangement reflected a desire for approachability and transparency throughout the project.

On one especially chaotic day I had reports to write so put my head down and insensitively ignored the need for proper greetings and warm welcomes. Instead I grunted replies to knocking at doors or windows and demands for instant responses. Three older boys came in and asked to see me. I grunted without looking up. 'Uncle', they said, 'look at what we found'. Again, little response until I heard a whimper and noticed they were carrying a bundle. 'We heard a noise coming from a skip and thought it was a cat. We got in and found this boy'. After that, nothing was more important than seeing three year old Joshua for the first time. He looked pale and sickly with sullen eyes and infected scabies covering his hugely swollen head. His tummy was bloated and he was clearly under-nourished and small for his age. He needed medical attention and protection before we could embark on a longer term plan. 'Skip Boy' was given the name

Joshua after a Biblical hero who showed great courage! He was outside the age range of children we ordinarily worked with and had expertise in so we embarked on a plan which would mean working with and through other agencies better suited to help him. He was initially placed at a partner organisation but in the care of a lady who, like Joshua, was HIV positive. Joshua's mother had probably abandoned him either because of fear or stigma or because she was in the later stages of HIV related illness. At last anti-retro viral treatment was becoming more available and Joshua was accepted on to a day programme at Mildmay a centre for care and treatment of HIV/AIDS related illness. Mildmay became a three way partnership between us and a peer organisation (Dwelling Places). Dwelling Places would have been described as the 'lead agency' and our involvement decreased as theirs developed. At a joint Christmas event five years after we first met, Joshua played a lead role and was striking in his waist coat and bow tie. A further five years on still and he is a healthy and happy 14-year-old at a fourth agency who are even better positioned to help him at this stage of his life. Extensive contact remains with Dwelling Places and some with the nurse in charge from Retrak Uganda. So there has been continuity despite agencies sharing responsibility. It is a good example of groups recognising each others' strengths and not being possessive about the children they work with.

Such collaboration does not come easily especially when rivalry or perceived competition for funds gets in the way. In 1997 I became frustrated at the failure of organisations to put aside differences and suspicion and work together. Attempts were made by the city council to bring NGOs together but there remained a deep suspicion about agendas and some fear of government and authority which was understandable given the background and context. When meetings were convened those who were willing to overcome suspicion and fear gathered but time after time had to wait in bare, ill-lit corridors for whoever had been assigned to chair the meeting. Conversation began to flow while we waited and after repeating this experience several times those that had come decided we would meet instead at one of our sites. There was a common desire to come together and talk, to share and to learn from what each other was doing. That was how the Inter NGO Forum in Kampala began. The five or six groups that began to meet in 1997 agreed it should be primarily for those who work directly with street children rather than those providing support services, working with other categories of children or from donor agencies. We also resolved to focus on issues facing practitioners – what is and what is not working and to create an environment where it was OK to say that something had not gone to plan. The intention as expressed in our initial literature was to learn lessons and find opportunities to collaborate. After three years it had grown to 22 organisations meeting every month and although like all groups there were highs and lows, at its best we were a group of peers offering support and accountability to each other.

Summary

From informal conversations and relationships built, referrals were made between NGOs, joint events and tournaments were arranged and we became a stronger voice to those in authority.

In time we would be invited to take part in forums, to design a manual for best practice in working with street children and to collaborate with government in some initiatives. The forum had a role to play in advocating for the children that we were all working with and to redress imbalances, inaccuracies and assumptions made in the media. It demanded and nurtured holistic ways of thinking – that together we were greater than the sum of our parts. We had far greater impact by standing alongside each other in the way teeth with no gaps can really bite meat!

3 A Relational Approach

Introduction

> *Relationships are crucial; it's not about structures, it's about making it work out there for children.*
>
> Lord Laming, 2009

Semakula Mawadri was a formidable goal keeper – probably the best in the first decade of Tigers FC. At times Mawadri was a positive presence at the Clubhouse, on the pitch and at special events for older lads. For a time he settled into a Tigers room while training as a welder. At other times his behaviour was disruptive and he seemed to enjoy sapping the energy of already weary frontline workers with constant demands. An opportunity arose to renew contact with Mawadri's relatives when we were travelling near their village and he agreed to accompany us. The visit was awkward as it soon became apparent his father would be furious if he discovered that Mawadri had re-appeared after many years away from home. As we returned to Kampala, Mawadri vowed never to go back. During the months and then years that followed he became resistant to opportunities that arose through the project. However, the relationship between him and staff was strong and although he did not respond in ways that meant we could tick a box or say he had completed a specific programme or reached a certain level, the trust between him and two of the social workers grew. Three years later his father died and it immediately transformed the situation. We had witnessed and remembered the circumstances at home and understood the importance of reconnection as soon as possible after the death of his father. It meant he could return to the village, restore the relationship with his mother and claim entitlement to a share in the family business. In Kampala we lost a superb goalkeeper but we heard of an upturn in fortunes for the football team in Mawadri's home village! He remained in the village and visited us twice a year.

This is an illustration of an outcome influenced by trust, continuity, perseverance and flexibility which are features of a relational approach.

Two decades earlier in a different but equally challenging part of the world, the following incident occurred when I worked as a residential care worker in a therapeutic community for recovering heroin addicts.

> 'Just get Carol to the car, push her in and sit on her! I'll drive off and shut the door once we're on our way. Oh – and hold on tight.' Once Linda had successfully carried out my orders, we sped through the estate, onto Easterhouse Road – when I managed to lean across and slam shut the passenger door of my old Renault 5 – and, ignoring all speed restrictions, back to the M8 towards Edinburgh. It was a hairy escape. I felt a failure.

An hour earlier, after escorting Carol to the Sheriff's Court in Glasgow, I had been persuaded – charmed even – into driving Carol and Linda to their home area. Both girls were on supervision orders to the rehabilitation centre where I worked. I knew about conditions they lived in at home and social pressures they faced. I was impressed with how they had performed in court and was relieved and a bit elated that the ordeal was over. Yet all residents were forbidden, until a certain stage in the programme, from any contact with friends and relatives who may derail the process. Carol begged me, 'Go on, let me phone my ma so I can nip in and see her'. To allow her was a stupid mistake. In a confusing series of events, Carol did not enter the telephone box. Linda stood between it and the car – preventing me from seeing. I discovered later they had been arranging this all day – and this was long before mobile phones enabled such planning! Instead, Carol went to a pre-arranged appointment with a supplier of exactly what she wanted that day – methadone – an alternative to heroin and a prohibited drug. Taking it would jeopardise the progress made back at the centre. When I realised I had been and was being tricked, a chase broke out and I persuaded Linda to get Carol and then coax her to the car. I was shouted at and called the most incredible things all the way back to the east coast but was happy to be returning with the same number of residents I had left with several hours before.

The following morning, the conversation with the director of the centre was a significant one I will never forget. Incidents like this, involving a zealous but naive residential worker, were not new to the long serving and wise head of home but I knew it would be a tough meeting. At the end of an in-depth analysis of the day before and why we had not returned until late, he leant forward and said: 'Andrew today you have learnt the difference between befriending and being a friend. It's a paradox – the residents are not your friends although your work is based on friendship. When you learn to combine friendship with professional judgement you will be an excellent worker and be able to offer something meaningful'.

Relational based social work

Although the above example occurred more than 20 years ago, achieving the balance referred to remains a challenge. Effective social or key workers need to combine strong and meaningful relationships with professional judgement. Developing skills to do that was an assumed and integral part of the social work training I went on to in 1989. For 15 of the 20 years after qualifying, I lived outside the UK. The current renewal of interest in 'relationship-based social work' reflects the way it was overshadowed by a managerial approach in that period. Attention to targets and performance-indicators has reportedly been at the expense of relationship in professional practice. My view is that without relationship there is no social work. There are no short cuts. A relationship is inevitably full of potential conflict and tension and can be draining and complicated but it *has* to be there for social work to have any lasting value. Relationship-based social work is the core of a broader relational approach to working with street children. A relational approach in this context is not about kinship or relatives but is about emphasising the importance of relationships. It is one which locates motivation and drive in forming and sustaining relationship, recognises much of human behaviour is about recreating relational patterns and acknowledges it is possible to establish healing or helping relationships which are wholly professional.

Relational leadership and culture

Relational aspects and ways of thinking must extend beyond the frontline 'helper-helped' relationship and pervade every aspect of a childcare organisation if it is truly relational. Leadership which is relational will influence the entire organisation. Walter Wright examines leadership literature and describes leadership as a 'relationship of influence'. His findings are especially apt for street child organisations when he states:

> A relational approach to leadership . . . has emerged primarily because it works. It treats people with **dignity**, offers **hope** and gives **meaning**, but the bottom line for most organisations is that it has proven effective in addressing the organisation's mission.
>
> Wright, 2000 (my highlights)

It is apt because street children are in need of dignity, hope and meaning. Some readers may be trustees or non-executive directors with responsibility for guarding an organisation's culture. Leaders model behaviour to followers so if your culture is going to be relational, find leaders who are relational in the way Wright and others describe. Covey portrays different types of power in leadership and links it to honour:

> Power is created when individuals perceive that their leaders are honourable, so they trust them, are inspired by them, believe deeply in the goals communicated by them and desire to be led . . . What a leader is beyond what he can do to or for followers, ultimately determines the depth of legitimate power he has.
>
> Covey, 1992

Consequently, relational leaders and workers recognise that:

> Protocols, structures, procedures and systems should take their place to serve, protect and strengthen the relationships that underpin a 'relational approach' rather than the other way round.

It was no surprise when an advisor commented that relationship was the water our organisation swam in. We nurtured a relational approach from Board level through to frontline staff and amongst street children themselves. It shaped recruitment, training and dynamics with authorities, agencies and peers. It is easier to write about than put into practice but this chapter offers a starting point by exploring trust as a foundational concept and six key elements of relational work with street children.

Key concept of trust

'Few delights can equal the presence of one whom we trust utterly.' George MacDonald wrote of trust in the 19th century but a relationship-based key worker in an organisation committed to a relational approach can enable street children in the 21st century to experience such a delight.

Trust is at the heart of relationship-based social work. It is a powerful force in any relationship as it creates confidence and reliance and produces certainty. Some street children have never been on either the giving or receiving end of trust. Some have been unwanted since before they were born into a world of uncertainty. They have been continually let down by those they should have been able to rely on.

Seven year old Eric had the ability to disrupt a staff team meeting with his high pitched whining or screaming fits in the courtyard of the drop in centre. This continued for his first few weeks at the Tigers Clubhouse as he perceived almost every comment and action by staff or other boys as hurtful or threatening. He trusted no one and had a fixed scowl across his face. Like many that particular rainy season, he was a victim of a cholera epidemic that swept the city. Emergency camps were set up by Medeçin Sans Frontières and other agencies and a visiting French doctor found Eric at the side of the street in a critical condition. He was treated and nursed back to health but had nowhere to go once the camps were dismantled. Someone directed the doctor to Tigers Club and he was left in our care. With the police we traced one relative, a violent uncle who had reportedly physically abused Eric. Eric's behaviour and subsequent information backed that up. In a setting with limited scope for police or court intervention, we took Eric in at his uncle's request – or rather demand! Several years later, Eric's early experiences of deprivation and abuse would manifest in challenging behaviour and low self-esteem.

It took persistence by one particular frontline worker to enable Eric to trust anyone. He repeatedly ran away. The ensuing search and being brought back to the Clubhouse were felt by the worker to be Eric's way of testing him out. It happened six or seven times in a four month period. Eventually he did settle and a foster family was found who later presented him with the gift of a goat. It gave birth to two kids and Eric insisted on naming them. The first he called Blackie because it was black. When I asked him about the second one he said, 'This one is smaller and not so healthy but I called him 'Eric' because he is the more beautiful of the two!' It was significant that this young man's sense of self worth had developed to that extent. Within a relationship of trust he was able to begin valuing himself. His talent for drama and unique personality developed and flourished, and in due course he would trust others with memories and insights into his own background and experience. Others began to afford him trust too.

Trust and its associated quality, respect, cannot be engineered or manufactured. The following stages or guidelines are fundamental to the process of earning trust and respect and foundational to relationship-based work which brings about positive and lasting change.

Entering the world of street children

'Please let us develop the photos first!' I pleaded with the earnest teacher who delivered 12 disposable cameras to the project. 24 street children were to be sent in pairs to photograph a day in their lives and the results sent to England for groups of school children there to study. In exchange, UK school children would photograph their lives and send us the pictures. The coordinator wanted undeveloped cameras to be sent to the UK for the children themselves to develop giving an immediacy and authenticity to the project. I felt the risks were too many and too great; there were child safeguarding issues around the use of images, there was a risk that any hitch in the process might mean the children who had taken the pictures would not receive copies, there were risks to the organisation if photos of activities in the slums had not first been checked by us.

I won the argument and we agreed that two sets of prints would be developed in Uganda, one for sending to the UK and one for children to keep if they wanted to. I collected the pictures and the first photo in the first set I examined was evidence enough that we had done the right thing. It was of a small group of children gathered around a pile of rubbish. On top of the pile was the recently deposited body of an unborn child. It was a gruesome image that would have stuck in the mind of a child in Year 6 in the UK for a very long time. Of course we should open the eyes of children to the world around them but in a way that is sensitive to their age and maturity. The picture depicted one part of a day in the life of a street child. Most of the other photos were positive and vibrant images although there were several of naked children washing in muddy water and a good few of gestures that may have been misunderstood or deemed inappropriate in citizenship classes in England.

The first photo reminded me of a time four years earlier when Bosco, the first Tigers FC footballer that we were aware of to become a dad, was forced to bury his two-month-old child. The baby died of TB and the only piece of land that Bosco and his girlfriend could afford was next to the mountain of rubbish in the heart of the slum. Standing with them felt like being in or watching a film. In fact, we were entering the very real world of street children.

Entering the world of street children means going beyond an academic understanding to a broad and deep knowledge gained, if possible, through firsthand experience. Observation and even more so experiences and interactions, no matter how ordinary or every day, will become points of reference to enable us to quickly understand and evaluate what information children share with us.

Setting aside time for reflection about our experiences consolidated the process and benefits to our practice. We included reflective work in our staff meetings and team development and aimed to deepen our awareness through role-play and other exercises to explore the world of a street child in as many ways as possible. It could be described as 360 degree reflection. We considered the senses – the sights, sounds and smells of the street. In our memory and imagination we put ourselves in the clothes and shoes of a specific child. We considered how a child walked and why he carried his feet or hung his head in a certain way. We spoke as he did – in a sensitive way not as imitation – to consider any peculiarities or possible delays in speech development. We re-imagined the smells on and around the child and considered their origin and what the response of others may be to the smell. In short we were asking ourselves, what was it like to *be* him? What was it like to live from one moment to the next with the uncertainty of finding food or shelter? As street child workers we had all witnessed children playing in drains of open sewage and eating grub infested remains. We tried to feel the pain of hunger, the dryness of thirst, to imagine his fears and dream his dreams. What about faith and spirituality in a context where spiritual realms are regarded as real as the physical? Some boys had been used in rituals while others claimed to have been visited by ancestral spirits. Some had a vibrant Christian or devout Muslim faith and others a simple awareness of their religious background. Inevitably we had to enter into the world of verbal, physical, emotional and social abuse and ways the child may protect himself from it or its effects. Street children were frequently spat at and in almost every city in the world there are labels given to them. In Kampala, labels included 'bayaaye' or the singular 'muyaaye' which apparently originated in the Amin years in reference to unemployed and disillusioned former soldiers – young men who were felt to be a nuisance. The words' origin was from 'wild cat' conjuring an image of an unwanted, dirty, scavenging creature. It became used of any 'thugs' and of street children in general. The experience of being labelled in a derogatory way was considered in depth. We witnessed people putting up their car windows, despite the scorching heat, as street children approached them and wondered how this continually repeated experience actually felt – their presence being shut out and their voices unheard.

Hot-seating (where a staff member remains in the character of a street child he or she has chosen) was a chance to question widely and deeply about likes and dislikes, what makes a child laugh or cry, memories, fears, friendships, who his heroes and enemies are, beliefs and hopes.

Equally powerful was the experience of devising theatre with street children. In 2007 we celebrated 10 years of registration in Uganda and one group of street children staged 'Home Street Home'. They pooled their stories and imagined the story of one child. It was portrayed with energy and humour but revealed harsh realities of intimidation, fear and loneliness. Humour was used to great effect as an older child urinated (with a well hidden plastic bottle!) over another while he was sleeping. The boys watching laughed knowingly. At other times in both Uganda and Ethiopia we used creative writing and art to enable children to allow others to enter their world. I mentioned earlier the poetry written by former drug users to fully express the depth of relationship they had with the drug. As they personified what to non-users is white powder, its power and hold were depicted and outsiders could enter their world and sense what it is to truly crave.

In Kampala, groups of street children formed 'depots'. Prior to a government programme to disperse and remove street children, depots were easily identified locations with characteristics of their own – some had been established longer than others, had definite leaders, attracted specific age groups or lads who showed initiative in certain areas (legal or otherwise). Individuals were known according to which depot they were associated with so even before learning names and building relationship, we knew a certain amount about them. The *golf course boys* had enterprises in horticulture, rabbit and duck rearing. They had a chairman and were a well-established group – a natural support network. Identifying leaders and building relationship with them were essential to understand a particular network. Leaders are people with trusting followers and it was important to discover why and how some earned the quality we mentioned in the last section; trust. The 'chairman' of the golf course boys was physically able to break up fights but the boys told us more importantly, 'alina amageezi', which means he has wisdom. He had uncanny ability to settle disputes. In a context where survival is the number one priority for each young person every day, it was fascinating to see how much the other lads trusted him with the little they owned, with cash and with information about their lives. The *Equatoria boys* were named after the hotel they lived in the shadow of which backed on to an area renowned for selling second hand car parts and commonly known as 'Japan'. Some of the boys were established suppliers for Japan. Others lived in depots close to rivers, near the bus station or close to the run down football stadium where kiosk owners would allow them to stay in a lock-up Coke stall in return for protecting stock. All cities have equivalent areas which workers should get to know well.

Mapping the area is essential to help you enter the world of street children. Initiating or facilitating a study is time well spent. A student mapped out the street child population in our area and researched mobility and the reasons children distributed themselves in certain ways. Resources about mapping are referenced at the end of this book.

It is possible to enter the world of street children and this section has outlined some ways of doing so:

- Respectful observation.
- Every day encounters and conversations.
- Becoming familiar with street language.
- Photo projects with the risks taken into account.
- Team development exercises including 360° reflection, feedback and hot seating.
- Noting social attitudes and significant labels given to street children.
- One-off experiences or significant events.
- Creative activities such as art, song writing, devising theatre and poetry.
- Regular visits, both day and night to the place they consider theirs.
- Identifying, respecting and relating to the leaders of natural support groups.
- Locating and mapping or facilitating research into spacing and mobility.

Engaging with street children

This section describes activities and programmes but first considers principles and concepts which increase effectiveness. *Engagement* as a concept seems to have gained popularity in social and youth work spheres but has the potential to be another buzzword without much substance. It is the process, as varied and irregular as any in social work, of going beyond encounter and into relationship. In the UK, detached youth workers identify ground rules of engaging young people; young people themselves enter relationships on a voluntary – not contractual or obligatory – basis and on their own territory. Detached youth work is not centre or programme-based so the aim of engagement is not 'outreach'. In Uganda, our ground-rules of engaging with street children were similar to those mentioned but the aim was outreach – to enable them to discover options available to them at the centre or through programmes being developed.

Our outreach had five strands of activity (see diagram on page 15) – *street work, medical work, football, feeding and work within the juvenile justice system*. Before examining those it is important to consider context. The social, cultural and political context, human and financial resources, nature and stage of project development are all variables that determine the most appropriate and effective forms of outreach.

For example, some cultures accept begging more than others and the religious context or worldview may implicitly encourage it. These factors create a very different street environment to contexts in which begging is frowned upon or even punished. In Addis Ababa and Kampala, our two main operational areas, we noted contextual differences.

During the early to mid nineties in Uganda, there seemed to be an intense desire to blame someone for the existence of children on the streets. There was media frenzy around this when we first arrived which seemed to fuel public opinion that children were on the streets because they had been bad or deserved it in some way or because NGOs had supposedly lured them on to the street. The Inter-NGO forum mentioned earlier analysed hundreds of press reports and found that almost every article used negative language about street children and many sought to end the 'problem' of street children. In that context, street work had to be carried out sensitively to prevent people believing allegations that NGOs were enticing children to the streets. That resulted in a joint statement to press and government that the forum did not tolerate the kind of 'unconditional handouts' described below.

Groups in Kampala, often from churches or faith-based organisations, began distributing food at key points. Some had hidden agendas or motives whilst for others the provision of food was an end in itself. Even when intentions were good, we were concerned for two reasons; firstly, children were perceived as better off because of these efforts and perceived to be running away from home in bigger numbers. In all the narrative accounts we ever received I can only think of one or two children for whom this *may* have been true. Feeding programmes came and went. The bowl of soup or bread (or even occasional meat) was never enough to account for a child leaving home and community and enduring harsh conditions on the street. The second cause for concern was that children who were receiving food were rarely, if ever, directed to an agency able to address deeper needs and offer longer term opportunity and options. These were 'unconditional handouts' and an example of a non-relational approach to work with street children. We distanced ourselves from them.

In May 2002 a government-led initiative to remove street children from city centre areas, including some of the depots mentioned above, was started and that had a massive effect on the extent and nature of possible street work. Government claims to have 'solved the problem', once children no longer harassed every passer-by going into the post office or bank, would have been weakened if street work continued in the way it had before. We were told it was no longer necessary to have a presence on the street and for a long time had to heed this instruction and adapt our approach accordingly. In collaboration with GOAL Uganda we maintained a presence on the streets both day and night through the 'Baaba Project'. Baaba is Luganda for older sibling and the project trained and facilitated former street children to be baabas or mentors to engage with children still on the street. It aimed to raise awareness of HIV/AIDS and more broadly to offer health education and guidance in the areas of hygiene, relationships, decision making and life choices. Under that banner we continued to engage with children in a less overt but equally effective way.

In Ethiopia, on the other hand, there is more tolerance of both children and adults surviving on the streets. Although there isn't a caste system as in India, the heritage of the orthodox church assumes that for some people street life is their destiny. On days set aside to honour, please or appease certain saints, followers are encouraged to give generously. Street-dwellers need to be easily seen on those days – of which there are many. Of course there were incidents where street children suffered at the hands of the authorities especially if their presence was unwanted during elections, when dignitaries were in town or when numbers of hawkers rose above a certain level. To be effective and sustainable, outreach and street work specifically must adapt to 'fit' the environment and context or respond to specific events.

Street work

Street work has many aims and can take on many forms depending on the agency, how street work relates strategically to the wider programme and on the context. Street work is often the first means of contact and plays a crucial role in 'gate-keeping'. This is the process of ensuring that children or youth for whom the programme exists are accessing it and those who fall outside the criteria of the target group are not. The effectiveness of other parts of the programme depends on good gate keeping and, if done well, it will enable an organisation to fulfil its vision. It requires careful planning and investing time and resources to get it right.

In Uganda, the purposes of street work were many; it was primarily to engage with street children on their territory, to introduce them to and inform them about the wider work of the project. It was one element of our outreach so it was not used primarily to recruit or boost numbers. It served to build bridges and assured boys at different stages that we were still aware of and deeply concerned about conditions on the street. It provided an opportunity to gain more information and insight and to verify facts and circumstances about specific individuals.

Project workers and leaders visited the depots mentioned above on three days or evenings a week either informally or for specific events such as clinics or meetings with the leaders or other individuals. Informal street work had no fixed agenda but was often the time when conversations and information-sharing happened, when we became aware of police or Local Defence Unit (LDU) activity, when boys were able to highlight new arrivals to the street, when we were alerted to a child who was sick or especially vulnerable in some other way. Here's one example from an early diary extract:

> A few weeks ago I met Jeremiah and Taban on the steps of Amber House. They are both seven years old and are very obviously malnourished. We have met several times since then

and they have generously given me their scabies! Jeremiah's scabies had become badly infected and his arms were covered in bleeding sores which have now been treated. The stench of benzyl benzoate in that quantity hits you in the face. It's been hard work getting their stories but they seem to trust us more each time we visit. They mainly want to play and Jeremiah becomes moody when it's time to leave. We have now traced Taban's father in Kasubi but he has not made any attempts to find his son and the team feels he is unable or just unwilling to care for him . . .

We will return to their story later. For years our street work featured a double cab Nissan van which was often hailed down by children and young people – sometimes because they wanted to jump on the back but usually for more serious reasons. It seemed important to offer a presence on a regular basis and children would tell us how good it was to see the Tigers van. The logo on the side was a guarantee that the car would not be tampered with as the children were keen to protect it. That offer was extended to Tigers Club supporters' cars when we introduced Friends of The Tigers Club car stickers!

There are many other examples of street work available in publications, on websites or through street child networks such as the Consortium For Street Children and 180° Alliance. One described in *Street Children: a Guide to Effective Ministry* is Covenant House, California (CHC). In that context, homeless youth are reluctant to access services or not yet aware of them so their outreach programme, which has reached over a million young people, is described as 'aggressive'. They have several minibuses going out seven nights a week when:

> *The outreach workers offer food, clothing and other help to those in need. This is done not only to help with immediate needs but also to build a trusting relationship with the youth that will hopefully encourage them to use CHC's other services and help get them off the streets.*

> www.covenanthousecalifornia.org in Kilbourn, 1997

In Addis Ababa, a serious consideration was the seasonal variation in numbers of children on the street. In times of drought or famine children came to the city in greater numbers than during the rains or harvest. It was important to respond in a way appropriate to seasonal street dwellers rather than bracketing them together with children who had run from situations of abuse.

Another variable is whether the city you are working in has defined entry points for street children. We were approached at one time with the challenge of developing programmes that could reach street children within 30 minutes of their arrival in the city. It was a donor-led request and fuelled by an understandably attractive notion of clutching children from the street almost before their feet have landed on it. It derives from excellent work of finding children who have made their way to cities on trains and buses and who can be quickly spotted and rescued before they are lured into street life. Organisations such as Railway Children work at stations across the world and do effective 'early intervention' street work. We defined Kampala as a 'final destination city' in that many children had stopped at or passed through smaller towns en route to the capital so came from literally all over the nation. However very few came in on buses and the train network hardly functioned. In fact, points of entry were almost as many as the children themselves. They would come on the back of trucks or by persuading drivers to give them a lift. Some came to the city with relatives who later abandoned them and others found their way by foot sometimes walking great distances.

Clarifying purposes, gate-keeping, our presence, and variables such as seasonal factors and entry points have been highlighted as significant in planning and developing effective street work.

Medical work

Clinics were held at three depots specifically for street children although it was hard to resist meeting the demands of surrounding slum dwellers living in appalling conditions. The project nurse and health volunteers dressed wounds, treated infections and administered basic medication. The team maintained excellent records – initially on old-fashioned record cards. Four years into the work it was reported:

> We have seen an average of 366 boys each month and 64% of these were under 15 years old ... More than 25% of treatments given were for wounds from hit-and-run type accidents, beatings by police or local defence units or from fights between themselves.
>
> Retrak Annual Review, 2001

Conditions were indicative of life on the street and the following were the most common:

- coughs, colds and fever
- wounds (includes bites, bullet or arrow wounds, cuts and burns) or abscesses
- muscular/skeletal problems
- respiratory tract conditions
- malaria
- fungal skin conditions
- gastro-intestinal worms
- eye conditions
- ear, nose and throat conditions
- genito-urinary disorders
- sexually transmitted disorders
- mental or psychological problems
- substance misuse – primarily solvents (*akagola*), aviation fuel (*amafuta*) or marijuana (*njaga*)

If conditions were serious, children were taken to doctors who treated street children with respect and without charge. This was an amazing provision and we remain indebted to them for diagnosing and treating often life-threatening cases. Serious conditions included TB, asthma, sickle-cell anaemia, kidney and heart defects, epilepsy and HIV-AIDS related illness. The lists of both major and minor conditions is worth examining and reviewing regularly to spot trends and to continue the process of entering into the world of street children. The causes and effects of these conditions will speak loudly of risks and dangers being faced, levels of hygiene and sanitation, behaviour and habits. For example, a local issue for us was the scrap metal business which created hazards for street children who were hired to find and deliver scrap metal to dealers. The incidence of cuts and back or hernia complaints after lifting and carrying too much of it was high.

Dealing with the effects of and issues surrounding drug and substance misuse is an inevitable feature of work amongst street children. For most children we worked with a change in environment and social work intervention led to a reduction in the use of substances associated with street life. In Kampala, the most commonly used and available substance was aviation fuel. A tiny bottle cost around ten pence and contained enough fuel to soak a rag and inhale for three hours. Effects ranged from a dulling of senses to hallucinations and in the words of one child 'it helped me forget where I was'. Other inhalants are common in other cities. In South Africa I witnessed children being taught to walk again after chronic long term glue sniffing had damaged their central nervous systems. Responding to substance misuse holistically entails placing it in context and dealing with it on many levels. It is not simply a disciplinary or medical issue but relates to lack of choice, understanding, self-esteem and environment. Other substances used included marijuana (*bhangi*) and khat leaves. A few older lads struggled with alcohol and a heroin based compound referred to as *brown sugar*. Addiction may need specialist advice, intervention or collaboration with other agencies. For further information and insights, toolkits dealing with substance misuse are referred to in the resources section.

Even when clinics had to transfer to the drop in centre, medical work remained a crucial element of outreach. As well as aims common to any medical service, it aimed 'to provide a welcoming and caring first point of contact'. The team noted that many children coming for the first time just wanted attention and to be heard by someone rather than diagnosis or treatment.

Football

Few global sports events have attracted as much attention as the FIFA 2010 World Cup in South Africa – and rightly so. Throughout Kampala, Nairobi and Addis Ababa street children crammed their way into video shacks to witness the rise and sad fall of African teams particularly Ghana. They then focussed on European or South American teams, cheering for and revering players as enthusiastically as children from those players' home countries. The Africa Cup of Nations which was similarly captivating. Screening key matches at the drop in centre was essential to maintain contact with the children as well as some of the staff. Initiatives inspired by the World Cup include the Street Child World Cup and a strategic alliance with 'Streetfootballworld' which led to a movement for development through football called 'Football for Hope'. In support of it, Kofi Annan said:

It is this passion for football that enables it to have a broader impact on the lives of millions around the world, particularly children.

Kofi Annan Former UN Secretary-General

With renewed energy for the role football can play in society, the FIFA President added his own comments:

> The driving force of our social engagement can and must be football itself. With its unique appeal and core values that reach across generations and cultures, football offers common ground for engaging in a wide range of social development activities . . .
>
> Joseph S. Blatter FIFA President

The thinking and vision behind these quotes echo the vision of those who first engaged street children by kicking a ball with them in 1994. Retrak has its origins in football – The Tigers FC – and evolved to be a social work organisation which continued to use football for both outreach and as a tool for development.

In Kampala, an open day of football training and occasional matches was held each week. Once understood that it was intended for those living day and night on the street, it attracted children and young people in big numbers. Within a matter of weeks over 200 were coming. The population largely regulated itself. If a boy who did not fit the criteria arrived for training, we were soon informed. A local primary school loaned us the use of their pitch and the training day became the focus of outreach for three years until more facilities were needed. The location was not ideal as some children had to walk long distances to reach it but it had advantages – it was away from the public eye which meant children could relax and treat it as their own and it was close to the Anglican Cathedral which initially provided free premises to serve food and offer basic medical services.

Although the football programme developed quickly and in time squads would compete in local tournaments and against schools, what happened by the side of the pitch was of equal importance to the lessons being learned on it. The pitch-side was a neutral environment for street children to engage with the staff, to build relationships in a safe environment that was as much their territory as anyone's and on a voluntary rather than contractual basis.

Rules during football could be enforced without any resistance but establishing rules during breaks and non-playing time was harder. Inevitably, there were thefts between the boys themselves and from volunteers and visitors too. There were many shouting matches too, which would erupt into fighting as the lads brought grievances, suspicions and divisions from street life to the pitch. There were times when training was suspended in order to defuse tension, and when the atmosphere was consistently spoilt by factions and fights, training was cancelled for a two month period. Challenges like these are the norm when engaging with street children. We brought the boys together following training to give them a chance to air their views and to give us a chance to make connections between what was being learned on the pitch and what we hoped for in the group as a whole. Teamwork, cooperation, trust and respect were all ingredients of a high performing football team so why not in life itself? Respect for property was fostered through ardently collecting boots and shirts at the end of training and delegating responsibility for carrying and cleaning them ready for the next session. Other types of positive behaviour were similarly reinforced.

The Tigers FC organised the Kampala Youth Cup for three consecutive years, for groups working with out-of-school youth. We experienced a sharp learning curve about the world of football as there was no shortage of challenges with results disputed and allegations of match fixing. However, it brought organisations together and provided a focus for the sports aspects of our outreach. National players presented awards which added to players' sense of pride and achievement. The main squad entered the national league tables and climbed steadily to the top of the Second Division. A difficult time followed when the core functions of outreach and gate keeping and the goal of reintegration into the community were being undermined or even threatened by the success of the football. That is an area we will reconsider in Chapter 4 which explores transition.

In Ethiopia, football was not such a central part of outreach. There were many out-of-school youth in the area surrounding the drop in centre that were hard to distinguish from those we were trying to reach and controlling numbers posed a real challenge. Staff team members used other talents and skills to engage with children. There were additional difficulties gaining access to local government land that was suitable. Despite those issues, football in other parts of the programme played a key role in relationship building and recreation.

Elsewhere other sports, theatre, art, circus skills or dance form part of outreach programmes in addition to street work or medical work. They may not have football's universal appeal but may be more appropriate for your context, skills and aims. Outreach activities should provide neutral territory, a sense of belonging and acceptance, learning opportunities and experience of team or community and enjoyment. All of that is in addition to the vital function of gate-keeping and introducing children to other aspects of the programme.

Feeding

To understand why we do things in certain ways normally requires an understanding of how they relate to the overarching vision. That was true for feeding. How often we offered food, why we did so on certain days or why we stuck to a specific menu are all answered by understanding the purpose of feeding and its relation to other aspects of the programme. In contrast to unconditional handouts already discussed, the 'open' feeding programme was part of the process of reaching out and engaging with street children. There was an expectation that children coming for food had been to training or had some reason – even if simply a dislike of football – why they hadn't. The food was served once football was over and was commonly assumed to be the obvious activity to happen after exerting so much energy. The need for sustenance after exercise is even more acute for children whose diets are irregular and poor. We progressed from water to pineapple or bananas to plates of food fairly rapidly in response to this very obvious need.

Juvenile justice system

Working with courts was a time-consuming but essential part of engaging with street children and entering their world. When there was a crisis or a round-up of street children, appearances in court were unscheduled. At other times they were planned and involved presenting background information or supervision records. The information resembled what were once called 'social enquiry reports' in the UK and enabled magistrates to understand the context of criminal behaviour and the support that would be available to reduce or end such behaviour. My background in the probation service was relevant and useful, but all key or relational workers should build rapport with the courts and acquire the tools and skills that would enable them to liaise not only with the courts but also with police and remand homes too. The Consortium for Street Children UK has produced an excellent work concerning juvenile justice (Wernham, 2004).

Key questions

There are many ways of ensuring street children engage with programmes offered. There isn't one right way of reaching out but it is important to know what your purposes are and regularly review whether they are being met. Principles are incorporated and illustrated in preceding paragraphs. Practitioners or those about to embark on working with street children should consider whether they are principles which could be applied in your context by answering some of these questions:

- Are street children and young people *engaging* with you and the project? Remember some features of effective engagement are that children enter relationships on a voluntary not contractual basis and on their own or at least neutral territory.
- Have you critically examined your *context*? There is no limit to the practice of ensuring your approach is relevant to the context. Context includes social and economic factors, the political landscape, attitudes in media and society, geographical location and movement of street children, particular needs or issues facing street children, seasonal variations, cultural norms and expectations, points of entry and the list goes on.
- What is your *presence* on the street? Children and young people themselves need to participate in helping you know whether you have a presence and how they perceive it. Is it regular and obvious enough to offer them security or reassurance? Does it counteract some harsh reactions of the public? Are you accessible and approachable? With increasing demands from children in later stages of the programme or from donor reporting requirements, it is often the ongoing presence on the street that starts to decline. Sadly, some organisations have no presence on the street and operate in an isolated bubble away from harsh reminders of street life. Having a presence has value for children who once lived on the street and for those who still do.
- Are street children and youth genuinely *welcome*? It is crucial that children feel welcome and wanted. That may mean ensuring team members prioritise greetings especially in hierarchical settings where the presence of children and even more so street children may not even be acknowledged. One organisation sticks to a strong principle of never taking before giving. Team members apply it to every area right from the point of first contact so they don't ask for a child's name before giving theirs. Warm welcomes – even when weary and facing

pressures – have the power to ensure relationships get off to a good start.

- Have you related your outreach or engagement to *longer-term needs*? Those who administer unconditional handouts should be open about it. I personally believe the purpose of engaging with street children is to enable new possibilities for them rather than simply meeting immediate need.
- Are those responsible for outreach activities clear on their *aims*? It will energise teams working on the frontline if they know how their work relates to the vision and other aspects of the programme. Activities may have intrinsic value but if they are part of fulfilling a bigger vision for children and their communities, their impact needs to be reviewed and measured in the light of those aims.

Forming authentic relationships

In the question about welcoming I used the word 'genuinely' deliberately. Another word may have been 'authentically'. Anyone with children of their own will know how perceptive they can be. A child can sense when something is out of the ordinary without necessarily having developed the ability to verbalise or link emotions to events. Many street children have an extraordinary ability to see right through people and to know whether someone is authentic. Like some fight or flight reactions to trauma or skills needed for survival, this ability may have been learnt through experiencing neglect or being continually let down.

In focus group discussions with former street children, some of whom had been given leadership responsibility, we were impressed by their ability to know before being told whether staff team members were trustworthy, reliable and genuinely moved by compassion to enter this work.

Perlman (1957) describes relationship as 'a catalyst, an enabling dynamism'. If such momentum or dynamism is not there, young people themselves know it. They perceive and respond positively to relationship driven by motives to enable or empower. If such motives are not present, the relationship is not authentic.

Being authentic in relating with street children begins with attitude. Our assumptions, state of mind, preconceived stereotypes, fears and motives all shape the way we relate. Critical self-review is needed as well as openness with other team members to give and receive feedback about the quality and authenticity of our interactions. This is especially true when we are under pressure or facing a particularly difficult encounter. Those are times when our personal characters are most evident and also when assumptions and other attitudes are revealed. Ugandan staff often reported how friends and neighbours could not understand why they were working with street children when so many other 'more deserving' children needed help and assistance too. It was good to air this but also to have the humility to admit when that thinking crept into our behaviour. Was that why we sometimes simply didn't bother to greet the children? Greetings are hugely important in everyday life in Africa and to by-pass them without very good reason indeed is disrespectful. Authentic relationship must involve respect.

Similarly, decision-making processes may have been clouded by stereotypes. This was a danger in a setting like Kampala where people from many tribes live and work alongside each other. Predicting how a street boy may react or making conclusions about why he failed to respond in a positive way may have been affected by assumptions or stereotypes about his tribal background. Whilst celebrating difference and seeking strength in diversity we actively discouraged such thinking. Authentic relationship demands an open and fair mind.

Cross-cultural issues

Working in a cross-cultural setting requires effort and careful consideration. Sometimes we are not aware of the 'baggage' we carry into relationships and sifting out what needs to be abandoned and what should be clung to takes time. Our motives may be utterly pure but until we are willing to get 'under the skin' or empathise with those we are working alongside, our relationships will not be as authentic as they could be. Empathy is a key ingredient of authentic, professional working relationships.

There are many examples of cultural baggage referred to ranging from gestures and behaviour right through to deeply held values and norms. Here are just four.

'Look at me when I'm talking to you!' was something teachers during my slightly shameful schooldays were often heard to say. Although the behaviour leading to that order was unacceptable, the crime was somehow made worse by avoiding the gaze of the teacher. Whether it implied arrogance, denial or complacency it added insult to injury and usually resulted in additional punishment. In an East African context we had to throw this baggage away. To look into the eyes of someone in a position of authority is regarded as insolent whatever the circumstance, so to do so when that person is exercising their authority is unacceptable. It is far simpler to pay lip service to the idea of changing our ways than putting it into daily practise. Non-national team members and volunteers involved in teaching street children at the learning centre found this one of many cross-cultural challenges to overcome.

Another example is the *use of laughter*. There were many times when visitors or volunteers struggled to understand why there was so much laughter at awful situations. In fact it was not impure laughter but a way of dealing with something, of release or augmenting a collective response to adversity.

Shouting is a taboo in Uganda and other African countries. Raised voices and intense, lively discussions are not uncommon as anyone who has travelled in certain parts of Africa knows. Shouting – whether at an employee or a street child – is regarded as utterly derogatory. It evokes fear and intimidation especially in a group setting within cultures where saving face is hugely significant. There is a Luganda proverb which reveals:

> *Awali engoma ennene, entone tezivuga!*
> When big drums are present, the small drums do not produce sound
> This suggests that when higher status people are around they can easily silence those who feel they have nothing to say or are intimidated.

A fourth example we struggled with was *demanding the truth*, which we regarded as paramount to build trust even when it hurt. In some traditional African contexts, I would argue that stating truth directly is regarded as less important than the preservation of relationship. To get to the truth often involved an elaborate discussion involving coded messages and what we regarded as 'going-round-the-houses' to receive full and accurate information. Time and time again we confronted this, both in direct work with street children – when what seemed to be straightforward lying was actually something quite different – as well as with staff teams – when keeping the peace seemed more important than giving or withholding information.

The list of national and regional cultural differences is endless as is the process of learning to work effectively with street children and colleagues in a culture other than your own. To do so requires authentic relationship and that takes time, effort and humility – but it's worth it!

Relationship with children in difficult circumstances

Authentic relationship between a worker and a child at risk or in difficult circumstances should also be:

- *Confidential within limits* – the child can freely share private thoughts, feelings, events and information and begin to make sense of them and how they relate to each other. There should be an understanding from the outset that information may have to be shared for their safety or in order to bring about positive change.
- *Safe* – the child must feel secure and that requires continuity, boundaries and predictability in the relationship.
- *Non-intrusive* – the child needs to know that the worker is joining them. In my experience the language of being on a journey is useful. Believing it's a privilege to join a street child on part of their journey adds an empowering quality and perspective to the relationship.
- *Purposeful* – in any social work relationship it is essential that the child or adult knows *why* they are there. It is easy to assume wrongly that aims and purposes are clear. If the worker is unsure of the aims, then the relationship will drift with little meaning.
- *Link the child's world and the worker* – the relationship should confirm in the mind of the child that the worker 'knows' their world. Entering the world of street children remains an academic exercise or something designed to fulfil some other agenda unless workers allow that experience to shape and inform professional relationships.
- *Special* – this is sometimes referred to as 'exclusive' but that could be misunderstood within a framework of safeguarding and boundaries. The child must know that there is meaning in the relationship to the worker. Building rapport may come naturally but there are ways to produce rapport and establish trust.

The list of qualities above and key points below are drawn and adapted from *Counselling Children* and *Counselling Adolescents* by Geldard and Geldard (2007, 2009).

Hearing and listening

Imagine how it would feel if your family and friends had no idea where you were. Now imagine you realised they didn't *want* to know. We all need significance – to matter to someone. It's a fundamental need reflected in Maslow's 'hierarchy of needs' which is often represented as a pyramid. The middle section is about belonging and is preceded only by physiological needs and the need for safety. Most street children demonstrate need in this area as their sense of belonging has been threatened or impaired. They may not have been listened to for a long time. A relational approach demands that we hear and respond to this need.

Many people comment on the vitality and courage of some street children. Some have a resolve and entrepreneurial spirit that is impressive and even admirable. Yet this impression, as well as the bravado and humour of street children, can be misleading. It is not the *whole* picture and an approach which is both relational and holistic requires workers who aim to see and grasp the whole picture. The qualities mentioned may be responses, mechanisms or skills acquired and honed in order to survive – socially and psychologically. For some street children, having them is the saving grace needed to pull them through or preserve them from harm, abuse and rejection.

This section is about hearing the story behind the picture. It is easy to listen to someone without really hearing. Some people think of it the other way round – that you can hear noise without actually listening to what is being said. We all know how frustrating it is to be talking to someone while aware that he or she is not actually hearing what you are saying. Something in their body language or tone of voice or in their eyes makes it clear that you do not have their attention. It can be blatant – such as the university professor who followed the path of a fly around the room while I outlined the latest chapter of my thesis – or it may be subtle. People in caring professions sometimes develop skills to give the *impression* they are hearing all that's being said. Children are often quicker and better than adults at detecting when they are or are not being heard. Tragically there are some who simply give up trying to be heard.

In 2004, a conference in Nairobi, hosted by Viva Network for Christian organisations all over Africa working with children at risk, was given the title *Hear The Cry*. Its basis was the Biblical story of Hagar and Ishmael – a woman and child who were cast out into the desert. At their point of despair, we are told in Genesis 21, 'God heard the boy crying' and responded firstly by addressing the need of the child's carer, 'Do not be afraid Hagar' and then meeting his immediate physical needs. The concept of God hearing a child's cry inspired those speaking and attending to fulfil His mandate by responding as He did. That starts with hearing the child. Delegates worked with former child soldiers, children who had been trafficked, child sex workers, children cast out because of disability and street children with backgrounds of abuse. Many of these children stop crying. Their cries fall on deaf ears for too long and their tears dry up. It may be only once a child has engaged with the worker, an authentic relationship has been established and trauma has been understood and is being attended to, that he or she can begin to cry once more.

With that in mind and before considering trauma, fundamental skills and methods to listen and actually hear the child will be examined. They are not considered in any particular order and interaction may include elements of all these skills. Playing, observing, active listening, asking questions and feeding back may happen concurrently.

Observation

In the course of all interaction – formal, informal, verbal or non-verbal, involving play or counselling – *observation* is vital to build a picture of or hear the child. Examples of things to observe and consider carefully are:

- behaviour
- general appearance
- mood
- intellectual functioning and thought processes
- speech and language
- motor skills
- play
- relationship with the worker and between the child and their peers

Active listening

The second skill in hearing the child is *active listening* to enable a child to tell her story and identify key troubling issues. The street child needs to know we are paying attention and valuing the information he is giving. Some of the elements of active listening are explained:

- *Minimal response or encouragers* assure children they have your attention and permit or encourage them to continue sharing information. If they are forced or unnatural they will be counter-effective. Naturally good communicators don't need training in using minimal response or encouragers. They happen naturally when we are genuinely listening. A simple nod of the head is a minimal response as are other non-verbal gestures, facial expressions and hand movements. Short verbal responses have the same effect. These vary across cultures so non-national workers should listen out for them and try to build them into their repertoire of listening skills. Some street children have been asked about their presence and background many times – probably in different ways by different audiences – so we need skills to ensure they tell a full and truthful story. Minimal responses are neutral and calm. It is important that street children don't read judgement or our own beliefs into our response. Some people are likely to say a loud 'wow!' or 'oh my goodness' or even 'you did *what*?' when they receive alarming information. These expressions will inhibit or distort a child's response to your listening.
- *Mirroring verbal and non verbal communication* is another tool which enables a child to relax and share his story and concerns truthfully. As with minimal response it only works if it

becomes a natural part of our listening behaviour. It begins with the worker observing and matching body language – how a child is sitting and moving, the gestures he is making In a gentle way the worker can mirror these with the effect of putting the child at ease. In the same way, matching the tone and speed of voice gives permission to the child to continue. During the course of conversation or counselling, the child will eventually start to mirror or match the worker's postures and voice. If the worker's posture is relaxed and their voice is calm so the street child – who may well have arrived tense, nervous, anxious, lethargic or fearful – will start to feel relaxed and able to speak calmly.

- *Reflecting content and emotions* is a technique which assures the child that they have been heard and, as importantly, the listener has understood what has been shared. One core aim of hearing the child is to enable them to deal with painful and emotional issues. To do that they need to be able to make sense of emotions, thoughts and behaviour. By reflecting on both what has happened (content) and what the child is feeling (emotions) links can be made between them. Reflecting content can happen by *paraphrasing* what has been said. Feelings or how a child has responded emotionally can and must be identified in order to deal with them. Linking content and emotions can happen through combined reflection allowing the child to confirm our response. Examples from our work with street children include:

   So you are feeling angry because your mother did not protect you from her new husband.

   or

   You were scared last night because you knew Katende thought you had stolen his money.

   or

   You become unhappy when other boys return home but you are still at the centre.

   These skills may seem blatantly obvious but they are often absent and it is worth reviewing how well we apply them in practice. In staff training we developed exercises to practise them and workers reported the different quality of information being gathered as a result.

- *Summing up* enables a child to start organising information so he can understand what has happened to him and the journey that he is on. It should draw out the main and most salient points that have arisen in the course of counselling. There will be periphery information which authenticates the account but may not be essential. All that has been said verbally and expressed non-verbally can be reviewed. The purpose is to enable a child to focus on resolutions and open his mind to new possibilities. The process for the child will be like this:

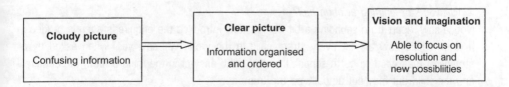

Cloudy picture Confusing information	→	Clear picture Information organised and ordered	→	Vision and imagination Able to focus on resolution and new possibliities

Asking the right questions

A third skill in verbal communication closely associated with active listening is *asking the right questions*. It may sound obvious but we have to let go of some features of adult-to-adult communication to get the quality of information we need from a child if he or she is to be heard properly. If you observe children playing together you will notice that they rarely ask each other questions. Of course this varies with age and maturity but we noticed it particularly among street children who had been traumatised or missed many years of formal education. Instead of asking questions of each other they often passed comment or made statements. In contrast, when a child encounters an adult she may be presented with a barrage of questions. Children in any setting will often give what they consider the 'right' answer to an adult rather than revealing what is really on their minds. Some street children we worked amongst were particularly adept at this – tuning into what adults wanted or expected to hear and responding accordingly. There was nothing wrong or alarming about this but if we wanted communication to flow and the child to tell his story wholly and truthfully we had to develop the art of using questions appropriately.

Street children are very used to interrogation. In Uganda, the law, which harked back to the English Vagrancy Act of 1824 disallowed children to be 'idle and disorderly', was still very much in use. It meant that street children were frequently stopped and quizzed. They were also the subjects of many investigations, research studies, surveys and reports; and so faced a stream of questions from people gathering data and information. In the same way donors and aid agencies carrying out feasibility studies or monitoring impact may well have a list of questions for children either on the street or as beneficiaries. Our desire as social workers with street children was to move beyond interrogation and into communication. It is easy to allow our agendas and lists of questions to direct interaction rather than ensuring it is led by the child's agenda and energy. Asking the right questions in the right way at the right time is one way of doing this.

- *Avoid closed questions* which at best may give you some hard facts. They limit or 'close' conversation and responses to them will normally be either 'yes' or 'no' or a one-word fact such as their name or 'fine'. They tend to start with Are . . ., Do . . ., Have . . ., Is . . ., Don't . . ., and examples in working with street children might include:
  - *Have you been living on the street for long?*
  - *Are you hoping to go back to school?*
  - *Don't you miss home?*
  - *Will you stop sniffing aviation fuel?*

  Notice how, apart from sounding a bit abrupt, they introduce the enquirer's agenda or ideas. It is incredible how almost every street child in the world will say 'yes' when asked by a stranger if they want to go to school. It is the 'right' answer in the mind of both the enquirer and the child but may not actually be the true one!
- *Avoid leading questions* which are even more of a hindrance to hearing the child than closed questions. These questions imply the answer more overtly than closed questions and may

inhibit a child particularly if they have struggled with people in authority as many street children have. Examples to be avoided include:

You got in to trouble with your stepmother, didn't you?

Things are not going well between you and the other boys, are they?

- *Avoid why? questions* as these seem to imply blame and may lead to a defensive answer. The street child will have been asked 'Why?' many times – sometimes with good intent and sometimes because they are being blamed for their own misfortune or others. If they feel they are being called to account they will resort to making excuses and be deterred from telling their story.

- *Ask open questions* which encourage the child to be 'open' as there are no 'right' answers. The answers will give more information and a chance for reflection. Periods of silence often precede more information in response to open questions and give the child a sense that their sharing is being valued. During a typical counselling session with street boys at The Tigers Club we sometimes waited for what felt like an awkward period of time before a lad really opened up. For some it was because they knew that we were not interested in the responses they had given to others. It may have been the first time someone had waited to hear them verbalise what had only been in their minds. Examples of open questions in work with street children may include:

  - *What happens on a 'normal day' on the street?*
  - *Tell me more about life at home*
  - *What do you think would be the best thing to do now?*
  - *How did you feel when they stole your clothes?*

  To encourage free narrative, open questions can include, 'And then..?' or 'Anything else?' or silence.

- *Add statements.* Reinforcing and reflecting what has been said helps street children to give comprehensive and accurate information. Simple statements give permission to the child to tell their story and demonstrate that you are hearing them. For example:

  'You must have been very brave to stand up to your grandfather' – after a child shares his experience of being beaten by his alcoholic grandfather, his strengths should be identified and affirmed.

  'When someone makes me angry, I shout a lot' – maybe in response to an outburst which was fuelled by emotion. A statement can give a child permission to have and express emotions.

  'I see that you have painted a huge cloud over the house' is a non-judgemental comment on a child's drawing which invites more information or explanation in a non-threatening way. Another inviting comment might be, *'I wonder why that cloud is so dark'*.

Finding and using creative tools

Active listening, asking the right questions and adding statements are specific skills in verbal communication with children but they are not sufficient on their own. Children will disengage quickly if we rely only on verbal communication. Signs of this are body language indicating boredom, lack of meaningful responses or no response at all. Another ability needed to hear street children is *finding and using creative tools* that enable children to communicate. These may include any or all of the following:

- artwork including drawing, painting, work with clay or construction
- games and toys for both observation but also to stimulate ideas and discussion
- puppets
- imaginary journeying such as the Road of Life
- books and stories which may free a child to say how they would have reacted to events
- symbols and charts
- activity worksheets
- drama and role play
- creative writing including poetry
- empty chair exercises that neutralise interaction by imagining a third character

In our experience these methods enabled children to express emotions, develop problem solving skills, improve social skills, gain a sense of achievement, strengthen communication skills and develop insight into their own experience. References are given at the back for resources and tools to facilitate effective communication with children. Workers should learn to adapt according to age and ability and be encouraged to practise and prepare well for using such tools. Children will give valuable information in creative ways if encouraged to do so.

Recognising and responding to trauma

This is a huge topic. Those working with street children will inevitably encounter the impact of traumatic events and need to be prepared to deal with it professionally, to invite specialist experts in or refer children to them. The latter requires humility and confidence and is not always feasible where resources or commitment to child psychosocial support are limited. Ability to recognise and respond to trauma must be developed and this was the primary focus of a cross-borders training event for Retrak and invited NGOs in 2008.

In other chapters, terms and words are identified that are easily absorbed into everyday language without being fully defined or understood. Trauma is another such word. Many projects claim to 'deal with' trauma or emotional wounds street children have. Tools that encourage creative means to enable a child to open up are commendable *if there is an understanding of traumatic experience*. It is potentially dangerous to open up a physical wound and leave it exposed. In the same way, additional damage can be done if emotional wounds are opened up and then simply left exposed or given the wrong kind of attention.

Defining and identifying trauma

The first stage should be to define trauma:

Diagnostic texts which offer definitive statements about trauma . . . lead us to conclude that there are two components to traumatic experience. First there must be an external event, in which the person is confronted with actual or realistically perceived threat to the life or personal integrity of self or others. Then there must be a response to the event which includes fear, helplessness or horror. Thus trauma is by definition a combination of an external event and an internal experience.

Cairns, 2002

This is absolutely critical in dealing with street children. Almost without exception street children will have experienced external traumatic events. Note that these can be to self or others. Witnessing domestic violence between parents even if the child is not physically harmed can be as much an external traumatic event as direct abuse. It is likely that a street child will have responded to a traumatic event with an internal experience which may result in trauma-related behaviour and emotions. However, do not jump to conclusions. The degree and nature of internal experience does vary and may no longer be an issue. If the child is now safe, has or had strong support networks, is at a certain age or stage of development and has been able to express what happened they may no longer be 'experiencing trauma'. We should not assume that every street child is at the same stage or in need of the same approach. A secure, authentic and potentially long term relationship as described in the previous chapter is the only context in which a worker can effectively assess whether a child is experiencing or has experienced *both* dimensions of trauma – external event and internal response.

There is no 'one size fits all' tool for dealing with trauma and we should be wary of any that claim to be. I witnessed children who had experienced traumatic events but who were stable and well, being counselled with a resource intended for those still experiencing trauma. Children's stories and experience must be valued and treated with respect. It is not *always* appropriate to encourage street children to share past hurts and memories.

More positively, street child workers equipped to recognise and respond to trauma should have a range of tools and resources available to reflect the spectrum of traumatic experience and the differences between children in terms of interest, ability, personality and resistance. So how do we recognise the internal experience of trauma? There are both signs or symptoms to look for and also strengths and attributes of children that may be absent. That's why relational workers with street children should understand development processes (portrayed in models such as Erikson's stages of psychosocial development, cognitive development and Bowlby's attachment theory) and patterns that transcend culture.

Children who develop in secure and stable environments without any major disruptions want to be with other human beings and have an intrinsic tendency to trust others. They will be attentive and responsive according to their maturity and development and able to interact with others socially. Children who have not experienced secure and stable environments may struggle with forming strong social relationships and have difficulty trusting others. Much research has been done looking at the impact of trauma on the brain and its functions. Trauma – an immediate event or lack of attachment – has been shown to restrict functioning in the thinking and problem solving part of the brain that also controls emotional responses. Challenging behaviour by children who have experienced trauma may have physiological roots we need to be aware of. It may relate to the body's natural defence system when faced with danger or stress. The impact on that system was manifested in some attitudes and behaviour we witnessed in our work with street children. Thea Wilshire sums it up as follows:

> *Reports on the types and forms of emotional problems among street children have included anxiety, attention and concentration difficulties, cognitive delay, conduct disorders, depression, destructiveness, developmental delay, learning disabilities, opposition and aggression, post traumatic stress disorder, school problems, sexual acting out, sexual identity problems, somatic complaints, substance abuse and suicide attempts.*
>
> Kilbourn, 1997

Those living and working with street children day in day out face the behaviour and issues described. It makes hard reading but is important to emphasise the complexity of challenges faced by street children. If you are embarking on working with street children it is important to go in with a clear idea of what lies beneath the often vibrant and cheerful surface. The following story has a tragic ending and illustrates behaviour and beliefs indicative of traumatic experience.

> Teachers at the learning centre identified the challenges Noah was having in the classroom and his lack of confidence more generally. Although he had a smile as wide as his face we didn't see it often. He was reserved and nervy much of the time. Our work was cut short one morning with the news that Noah was dead. He had been very low and reacted harshly to a security guard who moved him on from a nightclub doorway in an aggressive way. According to the other lads who witnessed what happened, the guard told him he might as well be dead. Noah replied, 'OK I'll die and then you'll feel bad' and lay down in the road near to the club. The first car driving past was a police vehicle. By the time they had got the body to the station Noah had died. Along with seventy street and former street children we buried Noah at the council cemetery. The boys rallied round with the preparations and those studying bricklaying built and designed a stone to 'Noah – our friendly guy'. We took the opportunity on the return journey to engage with lads about their own fears, about death and about who would care if one of them died. It was a fascinating discussion as it revealed information that increased our understanding and strengthened relationships.

Using the inner working model

Therapeutic social workers use the concept of the *inner working model* when referring to someone's beliefs and feelings. These are as significant as any behaviour and are seriously affected by experiences of trauma. These beliefs may be about self:

- *I am in danger.*
- *I am unlovable.*

- *There is something wrong with me.*
- *I am bad.*
- *I am the source of problems* (in some contexts this may be spiritualised with *I have brought a curse*).
- *I'm on my own.*
- *I have no control.*

Or they may be about the world:

- *I need to be on my guard.*
- *The world is not safe.*
- *No one knows what will happen next.*

One family therapist recently talked to me about 'children and adults with walls' in reference to those who had suffered trauma through long term neglect or even less overt insecure attachment in childhood. It was a useful phrase as I reflected on some of the street boys and youths who seemed so resistant to what was being offered, so indifferent to the possibility of relationship or so desperate to be in control. It is equally important for child care workers and project leaders to be aware of and address possible impact of trauma – in whatever form – on their own beliefs, behaviour and social relationships.

Responding to trauma

Having examined what trauma is and how to recognise it, this section considers some building blocks or elements of a response to it.

Create safety

I suggested that some children may recover from trauma naturally. If they are safe and stable, able to form strong attachments and express all that has happened the chances of this happening are high. It is possible to make sense of what has happened and to reframe it in order to face the future. The chances are reduced if strong networks or opportunities don't exist. Some street children we worked with formed great attachment with their new foster families or with relatives they had not previously lived with, experienced security and stability and, during the process of assessment and moving off the street were able to share what had happened. They made sense of the past and were able to reframe it in order to face the future.

In the previous section we looked at hearing the child and his story. When that story involves trauma, simply telling it can increase the level of stress hormones. That means children may suddenly stop sharing in order to avoid further memory-invoked responses. Workers should be attuned to this and ready to suggest a break or another activity. The environment and professionalism of the worker are core ingredients to this part of dealing with trauma.

The process of making narrative out of terror . . . can take place because being in a safe place among safe people allows us to take this little bit of memory and relive it safely, without crossing the threshold into being overwhelmed by the totality of the original disintegrative experience.

Cairns, 2002

Cairns mentions the words safe or safely three times. Street children need to know they are safe before they will share the narrative of their journey. When questioned about their past, street children may give versions of their story carefully adapted according to how safe they feel. In our context they were quizzed by police, local leaders, market traders, magistrates, journalists, researchers, donors and visitors to NGOs. It was fascinating to hear and read the range of accounts that could be offered by the same child and often there were elements of the truth in all of them. Only within the safety of a secure, professional and authentic relationship were they willing or able to reveal some of the emotional scars they carried from the past – the resentment, fear, anger, suspicion and sense of guilt. It could take months for social or key workers highly skilled in creating a relaxed and safe environment, for children to reach that point.

In terms of structures and programmes, many responses to street children create and ensure safety by establishing long term residential units away from the horrors of the city. A new environment is developed and a notion of safety is achieved. Such places offer refuge and the prospect of harmony although they can easily become so overpopulated that behaviour and discipline threaten both. Although appealing in many ways, creating an alternative environment in this way would have compromised the *transitional* aspect of our approach explored in Chapter 4. Being transitional entails commitment to empower children to thrive in their natural environment. When a child could not return to his village of origin he had to adapt to norms and face demands of life in a foster family some of which resembled previous experience. In the case of second-generation street children it is about transitioning rather than returning to mainstream community life. In both institutional and community-based approaches there has to be stability, security and safety to enable a child to start dealing with trauma.

Increase knowledge

There also needs to be an awareness or knowledge about trauma and its effects. It is not about excusing challenging behaviour but explaining it and dismantling some of the deeply held beliefs about self as listed above. So a street child begins to realise, 'Even though I do certain things it is **not** because I am mad or evil'. At the same time, street child workers and project managers must accept the reality and effect of trauma which means street children have needs that may differ from other children in difficult circumstances. Our criteria and indicators for measuring success must reflect that fact and we need allies and supporters who grasp it. It is why our response to street children was to work at a deeper level, for a longer period of time with a smaller number of children than if we had caved in to pressure for ever greater numbers. Action For Children capture the same intention in their carefully worded strap-line, *As Long as it Takes.* What a powerful message for donors who demand ever-increasing numbers of children to be 'dealt with' in a fixed period of time.

Understand feelings

Some children who have suffered trauma find it hard to understand their feelings and some become emotionally numb. It is a survival mechanism that we saw time and time again. The process of feeling and being able to recognise and name feelings needs to be revived. Games, role plays and activities such as 'eco-maps' or 'the Road of Life' are excellent for identifying events and the emotions that were felt at the time. Resources for unlocking information and helping a child make sense of what has happened and its effects are given on pages 156–7 . . .

Gain control

Street children who experience trauma, either before or whilst living on the street, may feel powerless. In contexts where choices and options are already limited, there may be little sense of self-determination or control over not just the long-term future but each day's activities and outcomes. Working with street children should involve offering alternatives and choices to street children and empowering them to respond in the best way for them. Alternative ways of responding to their own feelings need to be encouraged too. The rules at the drop in centre in Kampala reflected this. Rather than a set of Do Nots we asked the boys to imagine more positive messages. For example, instead of simply putting up a sign saying 'Do Not Fight', a poster was designed by a lad gifted at art with the strap line, 'When we are angry we don't fight – we talk about it'. Formal and informal counselling incorporated and reflected the same aim – to enable those still dealing with trauma to discover other ways of dealing with stress or challenges and regain a sense of control.

Fix the past

An old adage says you can't change the past but you can stop the past from changing you. This part of dealing with trauma is ensuring the past **is** past. It's the thinking behind many therapeutic approaches to behaviour change and addiction. Street children often face multiple and complex difficulties and ascribing negative events to memory is challenging. The belief that more bad things will happen may be deep and hard to surrender. Having a future focus is especially challenging in unstable or poor environments and the prospects of change seem remote in settings which embrace a fatalistic view of our position and destiny.

Change beliefs

We referred earlier to our 'inner working model' and the foundation of this is what Janoff-Bulman calls 'fundamental assumptions' or the beliefs that we have about the world around us and ourselves. Trauma – the event and the response – can shatter these assumptions and a child or young person may replace them with other beliefs. Each person involved in the life of a street child can help him or her transform damaged beliefs into constructive ones. Simply contradicting or dismissing negative beliefs alone is not enough. 'The key to helping the child to be free of . . . negative constructs is to *introduce choice*' Cairns (2002).

Many street child organisations aim to increase options and opportunities for street children, which is commendable but to enable a child to deal with trauma we need to increase the ways they see the world, those around and themselves. Some street children have 'heard' the message that they are unwanted from an early age or even before they were born. The message that they are of little or no value has been 'shouted' at them by all kinds of people from relatives to dismissive city workers. They may now believe labels they have been given – 'rubbish', 'evil', 'ugly' or 'guilty'. Possibilities must be introduced to provide the child with evidence that such beliefs are wrong. Affirmation and applause, healthy and loving relationships, realising they are not alone or that others face challenges too all contribute to a street child discovering his worth and bravely changing his beliefs.

Build positive relationships

Street children may appear to crave relationship and many visitors to our projects commented on how attached boys became to them sometimes within minutes. Less discerning visitors relished this attention and failed to recognise that blind trust can reflect deep insecurity. Other street children have difficulty trusting anyone and are constantly looking over their shoulder or reacting in a harsh way. Attention span may be very low, which is challenging for anyone implementing education programmes. It may take years for a street child to realise that relating to and with others can be a positive experience.

One aim of the halfway home (see diagram on page 15) was to enable residents to build positive relationships. Reviews and reflection often focussed on relationships with peers and residential care workers. They indicated how ready a child was to move on. In order to ensure the sustainability of a child returning home or being placed in a new family, they needed to believe in and experience positive relationships. For some children, such as Kinobe, it took much longer than the intended six months to do so.

Kinobe Moses was mute when we first met him. He showed developmental delay in many areas and was frequently unwell. As he settled at the emergency refuge, he began to make screeching sounds. Hearing tests concluded there was no diagnosis of hearing loss. His fellow street children were keen to teach him to communicate more. Kinobe's speech did eventually return but his behaviour continued to be challenging throughout his time at the halfway home. It became clear that he had suffered both physical and sexual abuse. He had been continually blamed for misfortunes in his home area and had experienced punishments such as being tied up with ropes and dragged along the ground. Kinobe had experienced trauma and even when an alternative to the street was found, workers wondered whether he would ever be able to build positive relationships and so create new and positive beliefs about himself and the world.

Boost confidence

Once beliefs are transformed and relationships built, the ground is ready for self-esteem to flourish. Encouraging street children to take personal pride in their work, appearance or environment perpetuates the process of developing self-esteem but also provides indicators for progress in this area. Clean up campaigns, inspections, incentives and rewards, providing facilities to wash both bodies and clothes, setting standards and examples are all ways we have found work. We borrowed an idea from a street child agency in Sri Lanka and installed full-length mirrors in key locations around the site. For some street children it was the first time they had properly seen themselves. Their impressions from looking in shop or car windows were not as full or clear as those in the mirror and it was encouraging to catch them unawares admiring themselves or trying the latest dance moves. Each cottage at the halfway home had a small plantation for boys to grow vegetables and fruit, which they did with pride. On occasions lads presented *their* tomatoes or cabbages or livestock which after careful cultivation and attention, were often impressive. Congratulations and thanks added to the process of nurturing a strong sense of worth, positive self-esteem and confidence.

Have fun

It has to be stated – children who have experienced trauma must have *fun!* After describing heavier aspects, it is important to stress that part of the therapeutic process is enabling children to rediscover and name joy in their lives. All social work is emotional work and has intense and difficult times, so embrace the times when recreation and fun are on the agenda. Games and tournaments, outings and visits, arts and crafts, sports and dancing are all opportunities to generate joyful experience. At residential camps for boys who were fostered we were not always confident certain silly games would succeed. We were proved wrong and the explosion of laughter meant they were often the most talked about parts of the weekend! The same was true of swimming in Lake Victoria, visiting a wildlife centre and even the airport – many lads had never seen planes on the ground and showed real delight witnessing take-offs and landings. Reliving the moments, keeping records through journals, photos and posters all helped to reinforce the positive work done on such occasions.

Constructing and testing a hypothesis: making an assessment

At the beginning of the chapter we considered how meaningful social work engagement involves both forming strong, authentic relationship and making professional judgement. The link between the two was made in the sections on hearing the child and on recognising and responding to trauma. This section deals with the purposes or 'ends' of relational work – to construct and test a hypothesis or several hypotheses and to make an assessment in order to take or facilitate action. Assessments and hypotheses were the raw material of the care planning meetings or 'barazas' discussed in the previous chapter and street child workers need to develop skills in forming or constructing them. A hypothesis is a theory which provides an explanation of facts and how they relate to each other. In relational work it is important to be bold and make a hypothesis. The hypothesis should then be tested against other peoples' findings and how the child himself reflects on it or responds to decisions made as a result of it.

In working with street children hypotheses may include:

- Why a child is living on the street.
- What occurred at home.

- What are the chances are of sustainable reintegration.
- The nature and significance of risk-taking behaviour (substance misuse, violent outbursts etc.).
- Reasons behind developmental delay.
- Reasons for inability to form strong relationships.
- Causes of a breakdown of foster placement.
- Reasons behind resistance to opportunities.

> *A social work assessment is an analysis of the ways in which various elements of a problematic social situation interconnect.*
>
> Pitts, 1990

The worker, who has observed, listened, interacted and responded to a street child, now needs to analyse all she has learnt. The aim is to understand background, personality, abilities, development, social relations, behaviour, aspirations and expectations and how all of these relate to each other. Being both holistic and relational in our approach is necessary to make a quality assessment. In order for assessment to be accurate and meaningful, it must (even where there is a managerial emphasis on procedures and systems) involve relationship and a holistic understanding of the child. Parker concludes:

> *. . . social workers must strive to engage with service users and seek a relationship based on exchange of information; a joint activity that guides the process . . . the underlying spirit of assessment concerns engagement and exchange.*
>
> Parker, 2008

Transference

Social and relational workers should understand the concept of *transference*. It is:

> *the idea that in our current relationships and interactions we may 'transfer' feelings into the here and now which actually belong in our previous relationships.*
>
> Ruch, Turney and Ward, 2010

It sometimes manifests as 'projection' and in everyday life and stable relationships may not be significant. Working with street children – like any social work – involves past hurts, difficulties, anxiety and insecurity. In that context it is extremely significant and workers, particularly those in counselling situations or who spend many hours with individual street children, need to develop skills in identifying transference and working with rather than against it. In our context, the emergency refuge warden, residential care workers or field social workers were those likely to encounter transference.

In a previous setting, I worked in an intensive way with children in an assessment centre. Had they been of criminal age, many would have been serving long custodial sentences. One boy had set fire to two schools and attempted a third attack on a home.

Matthew's behaviour was dangerous to himself and others but until the impact of trauma in his life had been dealt with, there was little hope of lasting change. His inability to control anger was one indication of previous experience. One of the most fascinating episodes of a relationship-based assessment was when that anger began to be 'transferred' into the here and now. At first it was generalised anger, then it was targeted or transferred to a specific school teacher, then towards a fellow pupil and finally to me as his key worker. He quite suddenly turned and began to 'hate' me and outbursts became difficult to manage. At one stage he set fire to the room we were in. In discussions with a child psychiatrist it became very clear that this was transference seen in an overt and clear way. After eight years of both physical and sexual abuse, Matthew was powerless and angry. Fire-setting was a manifestation of the need for power and control and his angry outbursts were transference.

A street child who has been constantly let down or treated in a hostile way by relatives may bring their responses to that into a healing relationship. It could mean they resist help with an unconscious question in mind – 'why should I trust anyone in authority?' Residential care workers and social workers in Kampala sometimes felt they were being pushed away or being pushed by specific individuals to test their limits. This was transference-related behaviour.

Counter-transference is when a worker or counsellor acts or reacts according to previous relationships or events. If a child is beginning to relate to you as if you are the aggressive parent, counter-transference is when you start to behave like the aggressive parent. In working with Matthew, it was important to de-personalise what was happening and remain professional throughout in order to prevent counter-transference.

It is not easy dealing with transference. It implies a level and intensity of relationship that is meaningful. Hurtful things can be said – like the time one lad told me I had ruined his life and he would have been better off not knowing me. He had benefitted massively from several areas of the project. The Ugandan staff encountered transference from hostile reactions by lads who had begun to trust them and open up. One group of older boys threatened to poison staff and their families at a stage when they were approaching 'graduation'. Rather than celebrating achievement, they projected previous thoughts and fears of abandonment and rejection onto current relationships with key workers. If you are currently working in a meaningful way with street children you will have similar experiences, so be assured you are not alone.

Summary

A *relational approach* to working with street children acknowledges the value and power of relationships. It is reflected in both relationship-based frontline social work and a whole organisation commitment to authentic and positive relationships. Modelling such a commitment is a duty of the Board to its executive leaders, of leaders to frontline workers and of frontline workers to street children themselves. After considering the key concept of trust, a relational approach in practice was considered by looking at six key elements or building blocks; entering the world of street children, engaging with street children, forming authentic relationships, hearing and listening, recognising and responding to trauma and the importance of assessments and hypotheses in order to plan for real and lasting change.

4　A Transitional Approach

Introduction

A transition is a journey or pathway from one state, form or place to another. A transitional approach to working with street children is one which enables a street child to find a pathway and travel the journey from one place to another. It implies that the organisation itself, its structures, programmes and relationships are not the 'destination' but are geared towards equipping a child to travel to a different state, form or place. The language of being on a journey with joys and struggles is a useful one. It influenced our perspective and reminded us that to walk alongside street children is a privilege. Being transitional implies a willingness to let go to enable former street children to complete their journey and reach their destination.

Any transition has to have starting and finishing points. In a transitional approach we must define those points in the life of a street child. Where have they come from and where are they heading? Answers may be either *concrete* – they have come from a certain area and family and are heading back to that area or to a new family, or *abstract* – they have come from fear and instability and are heading towards acceptance and security. Answers may be detailed and complex or straightforward. The principle remains – that the child is on a journey and we need clarity about the direction and certainty that the child is moving towards a defined destination. The level of support needed will vary from child to child, obstacles on the way will vary in degree and nature, there will be unexpected difficulties, surprise encounters and possible detours but the sense of journeying and momentum must remain.

We will examine what a transitional approach involves in practice after describing the values or beliefs upon which it is based. These beliefs are supported by a growing corpus of globally accepted research and practice-based evidence.

Transitional thinking

The key concept of family

> *Mwaana mugimu, ava ku ngozi*
> A big, healthy child gets his stature from the ngozi (ngozi is a cloth used for tying the child to the mother's back).
> This Luganda proverb infers that a child's growth and development depend on the nurture and care received from parents.

Child development happens within the context of interpersonal relationships. Generally speaking, a child's first experience of interpersonal relationships is in the context of a family unit of one form or another. Development that follows enables and equips a child to adapt to and thrive in their community during adulthood. That is why it is acknowledged universally that children have a right to grow and develop within protective and positive family environments. The Convention of the Rights of the Child (CRC) assumes that the family is the environment in which a child should develop whilst recognising the need to protect children in situations where the family is not fulfilling its role. Article 4 is primarily about rights to protection and participation and in relation to those makes references to the family which are summarised by UNICEF. I have highlighted the fundamental roles of family described:

> *Governments must help families* protect children's rights and create an environment where they can grow and reach their potential.

> *Governments must respect the rights and responsibilities of families to* direct and guide their children so that as they grow they learn to use their rights properly.

> *Parents are encouraged* to deal with rights issues in a manner consistent with the evolving capacities of the child.

> *Governments have responsibility to protect and assist families* in fulfilling their essential role as nurturers of children.

Quotes from Understanding the CRC by UNICEF

The International Save The Children Alliance cites the CRC as one of many declarations or frameworks to embrace the belief that parents or families have intrinsic roles and responsibilities:

> *The CRC and other human rights instruments emphasise the role of the parents. Parents or, when applicable, the extended family or legal guardians, have the primary responsibility to take care of, support and guide the child in a way that is in the child's best interest.*

Save The Children, 2004

Rights based frameworks, child development experts, proverbs across cultures, theological and faith-based perspectives all point to the foundational belief that:

> *Family – in whatever form – is fundamental in providing a safe and loving environment in which a child is able to realise their potential.*

It is why leadership expert Stephen Covey refers to the family unreservedly as 'the building block of society' and why politicians wrangle over who cherishes the place and value of 'the family' in society the most.

Sometimes our understanding of 'family' can be limited by what we are familiar with. What we have said so far relates to family in its broadest sense, across cultures and nationalities and in its different forms. The form, structure and size of 'family' are less important than roles and responsibilities which are determined and fulfilled by the quality of relationships. Psychologist HR Schaffer explains:

Surveying all (these) studies on the influence of family characteristics on children's development, one conclusion emerges clearly from the accumulated evidence, namely, that **family structure plays a far less significant part than family functioning.** *Structural variables . . . have been found to exert little influence on children's psychological outcome. Of far more importance is the* **quality of relationships prevailing** *among whatever individuals constitute the household – qualities such as warmth, commitment, mutual understanding and harmony.*

Schaffer, 2004 (my emphasis)

The emergence of long term residential care of children and its continuing prevalence in certain parts of the world was and is largely due to a belief that institutions can fulfil the roles and responsibilities of families. Institutions of many forms have become the 'destination' for the homeless or abused child. Much work has been done to ensure best practice in such centres, recognising there are inherent challenges to providing the environment needed for children to fully grow and develop. The Scottish Institute of Residential Child Care (SIRCC) exists to ensure that residential care is 'valid, stable, nurturing and therapeutic'. It recognises that for some children at specific times residential care is necessary but suggests, 'It will be a relatively small but core service offering specialised and expert provision'.

The purpose of considering the foundational value of family and the purposes of residential care is to enable us to find the best starting and finishing points of the journey in a transitional approach to working with street children. At this point we need to establish whether street children are in need of residential care and whether residential care offered is nurturing and therapeutic, specialised and expert. Is it able to fulfil the roles of family and home? Is it equipping children for adulthood within their community?

If your work already involves long term residential care – in whatever part of the world – research, resources and training available are crucial to ensure the service provided is the best possible. A few years ago, SIRCC partnered with some organisations in Uganda to offer training and advice which is universally relevant and in the best interests of the children we are entrusted to work with.

The reason for emphasising this is because there is growing evidence that much institutional care in many parts of the world is either unnecessary or putting children at greater risk than they were before. SCF's 'A Last Resort', referred to above, responded to concern about residential care by examining the effects of institutional care on children and their development:

The global use of residential care is often underpinned by a belief that if children are removed from undesirable influences in their homes or environment, given training, and subjected to strict discipline, they will somehow turn into 'model citizens'. Others believe that removal from poverty to higher standards of living in a children's home will bring lasting benefits to the child and society. Modern research on child development and the effects of loss, separation and institutionalisation on children have now challenged these assumptions.

Save The Children, 2004

The global perspective of 'A Last Resort' comes through information from dozens of countries. It takes a pragmatic approach and identifies the reasons why residential care is *unlikely* to be able to fulfil the roles of family-based care. There are so many variables and the reality of risks and violation of rights is shown in disturbing facts and figures as well as anecdotal evidence. The following quote, which appeared in the *Daily Nation*, a Kenyan national newspaper, was written by someone who spent most of his childhood in an orphanage. He shares bitter memories of a largely negative experience of institutional care before concluding:

Institutions are like zoos. People come to visit, play with us, then leave us in our closed compounds. In a nutshell, we're in cages. There is also the pity. I saw many visitors crying, and this made me feel bad about myself, and made me realise that I was really different from other children. They say it takes a village to raise a child, but show me how many institutions are community owned. Or how many are run or funded by Kenyans. Over 70 per cent are run by individuals, groups, and organisations from the developed world.

S Ucembe of Kenya Network of Care Leavers, 2010

It is often assumed that children who are in institutions need to be there and that there are no better alternatives. The truth is that many do not need to be there and there are better — and cheaper — alternatives to long term residential care. In Uganda, the Ministry of Gender, Labour and Social Development discovered in 1997 that 85% of children in 'orphanages' across the country had identifiable and traceable relatives (Save the Children, 2004: 16). In other words there are relatives in the community who, with support, could care for children currently living in institutions. Findings like these informed our planning and practice.

There are examples of institutions that try to model 'family' by putting children in smaller units with 'maamas' to care for them. Some of their facilities are impressive. However they remain institutions in that the overall numbers are large, the carers are still there on a contractual basis and in reality could walk out or be sent away tomorrow. Discipline, conditions and regimes vary and the sense of 'identity' formed with the institution is not necessarily healthy. Integration or reintegration into the wider community remains a concern and in my experience problems abound for children who have become so dependent on an institution they find it difficult to leave, settle or thrive in mainstream communities.

One institution I visited had 400 residents in family-style accommodation. Although it was being run well a few things concerned me — the first was the ban on local languages and insistence that only English was used in the centre. I wasn't allowed to converse with Baganda children in Luganda which felt strange and I wondered who was being served by this rule. The second concern was that staff did not know of any children leaving the centre to be reunited with relatives or even how many families had been contacted. This was the 'destination' so there didn't seem to be any urgency about making links with families or communities of origin. The third concern was the labelling of children. This is an 'x-child' (x-replacing the name of the organisation) was often heard both inside and outside the facility and I was told with pride that former residents or 'x-children' had given birth to 'x-grandchildren'. In contrast, children who passed through our programmes into foster families or to be reunited with relatives wanted to shed labels associated either with being a street child or being assisted by an organisation. They longed to be known by their own family name or given a new name by a foster family. It was with joy that we were told, 'I am no longer a "Tiger", I am now a "Kavuma"' or 'I am never going to be "muyaaye" again – I am now "Seguya"'. These statements symbolised the destination of integration, acceptance and belonging we wanted them to reach.

The concerns expressed are personal but highlight reasons why I am convinced a transitional approach to work with street children is almost entirely incompatible with long-term residential care. The only exceptions are when specialised and expert provision is needed but these are rare. The destination should be potential-releasing and protective family. I would never advocate returning children to abusive situations where they are unprotected and their development is hindered. Of course all families are flawed and 'imperfect' but accepting and working with those imperfections meant around 500 children were reunited with families or placed in new foster families in the first decade of the organisation's existence.

In 2008 we organised and hosted a one-day conference called 'A Home For Every Child'. It was the first advocacy event of its kind in Uganda and was attended by politicians, community and religious leaders, heads of NGOs, members of international donor agencies and journalists. The purpose was to advocate for family-based care, to inspire others with emerging foster care programmes and to challenge the assumption that institutional care was the only way to respond to the rising numbers of orphaned children. There were lively discussions and poignant moments during the day. The Bishop of Kampala wept when he was invited to speak and said, 'This is what we have been waiting for.' Another powerful moment was when an elderly statesman, who was influential in childcare for decades, stood up and challenged the High Commission representative. He implored the British and others to stop building yet more institutions and said, 'Like you, we want our children in families, so please stop!' Visiting social work experts and the representative assured him it was not mainstream thinking to desire more children's homes and orphanages. The point was made strongly that it is often faith-based organisations or those who respond emotively and with good intent to the challenge that still insist on bringing institutional care to Africa. Why? Long-term residential care is relatively easy to initiate and seems to offer a tangible and quick solution for vulnerable children. It appeals to some donors and supporters who want visible proof of the impact their support is having.

Many smaller organisations I meet and advise have a vision to build a children's home or equivalent. My challenge to them is to consider the long term sustainability of effective care in institutions, the inherent risks with so many variables, the often higher-than-expected costs of running and maintaining a centre and the points mentioned above about the limitations. On a more positive note, I encourage those considering or initiating programmes to:

- Discover good examples of groups that, despite huge challenges, enable children who would otherwise be in institutional care or on the street, to remain in their communities. There are hundreds worldwide but two examples are the *Zimbabwe Orphans Through Extended Hands* agency which enables over 70,000 children to remain within the community and *Chilli Children* which ensures 5,000 disabled children in a remote area of Uganda are accepted and supported by their communities.

• Get informed about family and community based care through research and information from *Save The Children, UNICEF* and *World Vision* or through the *Better Care Network* which offers global information exchange or agencies like *Substitute Families For Abandoned Children* which exists to strengthen foster care programmes in parts of the world where it is relatively new.

The key concept of community

'Community' has been mentioned several times already. Families exist within the context of a community. Most definitions of community emphasise sharing some or all of the following: tradition, intent, locality, government, interest, environment and language. It conveys identity, participation and inter-dependence.

Another foundational belief to the transitional approach we developed is that *The community has a vital role in the protection and development of its children*.

Community is so important that even when a child is separated from her biological family or when a family is unable to fulfil its nurturing role, family-based alternatives within mainstream community life should be sought (except in very unusual circumstances). David Tolfree of Save The Children explains why:

> *Family-based care is not only more likely to meet their developmental needs, but is also more likely to equip them with the knowledge and skills required for independent life in the community. By remaining within their own communities they both retain a sense of belonging and identity and also benefit from the continuing support of networks within that community.*
>
> Tolfree, 2003

What if a street child's community is 'the street'? Friends working with street children in Manila and Bogota wrestle with this issue on a daily basis and there is an emerging debate about street families and second or third generation street children who have never known 'community' apart from the street. Particularly in mega cities street children and families have created community and support networks amongst themselves. As Thomas Feeny points out in a paper commissioned by the Consortium For Street Children:

> *The reality is that forming 'surrogate family' groups is often a means of survival for street children, who depend on the sharing of resources and information to protect themselves and each other from violence and police harassment.*
>
> Feeny, 2004

A pragmatic response is essential to meet the immediate needs of such surrogate families and second or third generation street children. That may involve working with whole families and street communities while they are still living on the street rather than seeking integration or reintegration into mainstream society or community life. There are strong arguments for protecting street children's and street families' rights to remain on the street. I support and accept those arguments only if:

• By remaining on the street, children's rights to safety and protection, enjoyment and fulfilment are upheld.
• The right to remain on the street does not violate the absolute right to life itself.
• They are being socially and psychologically equipped for life as interdependent adults in the wider community.

Living on the street is, for almost every street child I have met, a negative and damaging experience. The street has been described as 'the devil's playground' because of its destructive impact and our experience reinforced that view. In stages of the counselling process when 'masks' were removed and tears shed, the extent and pain of that destruction was clear to see. Loneliness, fear, bitterness, grief, pain and anger – all from street life experiences – were revealed and often combined with a distorted, entirely negative view of self. Street life in most places brings physical danger too. In a nine-year period 16 children known well to our project died and many more suffered from life-threatening illness or severely infected wounds which would have killed them without the medical team's intervention. Every incident, sickness or death was a reminder of the stark and harsh realities of street life. In other parts of the world the situation is worse. Reports in the early nineties (*The Economist*, July 31 1993) suggested that few street children in Brazil lived beyond the age of 18 and a UK agency reported recently that, 'observers from our partner in Guatemala say that street children there have a life expectancy of around four years on the street.' www.toybox.org

In the face of adversity and danger, some street children do appear – at least some of the time – to 'do well' on the streets and I can think of many who are innovative and entrepreneurial. There is a spirit and ingenuity that comes from having to survive and thrive in difficult circumstances. However, I can only think of one out of hundreds that seemed safe and protected, realising his potential, socially skilled and wanting to live on the street. Known as 'captain' to fellow street children and members of the public, Isaac came to the project and was a positive influence on younger lads. He let us know if any were in trouble or of new arrivals on the street, fully appreciating that he was unusual in wanting to stay on the street long-term.

Of course some children *think* they are better off on the street and will repeatedly run back to the street even when there are alternatives but behind the bravado and camaraderie there is a longing for 'normality' or to belong somewhere and to someone. The discussions we had with lads after the burial of yet another of their friends have already been mentioned. I refer to them again because of their significance in relation to this chapter. One lad – called 'number 10' by fellow depot members – had not given any accurate information about his family and community for four years until one of his friends died. He began to wonder what would have happened if it had been him. Would he have been buried in the council cemetery? Would any of his relatives have been told? So he started to open up and others joined him in expressing deep fears. Some of them wanted to be buried 'with their people' while others said they just wanted their relatives to know. Information about families and villages began to flow more readily from these particular lads and real desires began to be revealed. The stories and aspirations told on such occasions or when tears are shed in counselling are the ones we must be ready to hear and respond to. Practitioners should remain curious even when a child says they prefer the street to 'home'. Of course some have come from situations of abuse and for now the street seems a better option. Yet the child who says he prefers the street to home is not necessarily saying they reject the notions of 'home', 'community' and 'family' altogether.

In Nairobi, I met 'street families' living in a web of underground tunnels beneath one of the largest city roundabouts. Here was a 'community' created by street children who were now producing the next generation of street children. Some of the tunnels were full of rotting waste and there was a constant threat from the council of having more rubbish dumped there. Clothes given to the children were confiscated on a regular basis by local defence units. I was shown the tunnel that some of the toddlers had been born in and where one girl would deliver a baby probably within the next week. The person who took me there had experienced street life himself. I commented on the group – how they had organised themselves and seemed to be making the most of a seemingly impossible situation to which he responded:

> But Andy these people have no hope – don't you see – they don't know how to hope, they have forgotten what hope means – they have nothing . . .
>
> Ronny – a former street child

It struck me then that even though the challenges of providing alternatives are huge and even though there may be strong networks formed by resilient street families, critical questions must surely be answered:

- Are we short-changing long term street children and street families if we don't strive to increase options and create choices just as we do for new arrivals on the street?
- Once there are alternatives and choices, are we equipping children and young people with decision-making skills appropriate to their stage of development? Do they fully understand not just the choice but the *consequences* of a choice to remain on the street – even if they are exercising their right to do so?

A transitional approach to working with street children should embrace the inherent values and responsibilities of 'family', in whatever form, and community. Those adopting a transitional approach should be ready to address the issues and answer the questions raised above. A transitional approach in practice will mean different things to organisations in different contexts. Agencies and international networks can offer a more global perspective than can be offered here. What follows in the five appendices to this chapter is an outline of transitional practice for our particular organisation in East Africa.

Transitional practice

Finding entry and exit points

Work with street children resists a formulaic approach and demands flexibility, creativity and spontaneity. However, we learned the hard way about the need to be as clear as possible in regard to entry and exit points to enable movement or transition to happen:

- *Entry*: In sections on street work and sports the 'gate-keeper' role was considered. When this function was not understood or maintained, other parts of the programme were affected and the organisation was hindered from fulfilling its vision. It is critical for an organisation working with full time street children to be certain the right target group is being reached. In both Kampala and Addis it would have been easy to water down our criteria in order to respond to the needs of thousands of extremely poor 'slum children'. To do so would have meant a shift in our reason for being there. What we had to offer was for a particular group of children at a particular stage of their journey.
- *Exit*: It is equally important that 'exits' are identified and established. Children moving out of and beyond the programme should be planned for and celebrated. We failed to recognise the importance of this for the first three or four years until we were forced to do so.

In 2001 we experienced a six-month period of especially disturbing and dangerous behaviour from lads who had been part of the lifeblood of The Tigers Club since its inception and had increasingly dominated our thoughts, time and energy. The group was about 30 young men who regarded themselves as *the* Tigers. Most had joined six years previously when they were 12 or 13 years old. Probably three times that number had by then moved into full time education or training, been helped to start a small business or reunited with relatives. Several members of the group had been on one or more of these programmes. For many and complex reasons they had not coped or responded positively to what was offered. They continued to benefit from medical care, sports and feeding. Those whose businesses failed or who were suspended from college or who were still caught up in substance abuse, fighting and in and out of police cells were given repeated chances. We failed to recognise that running back to Tigers Club to be given yet more chances was a pattern that would be increasingly hard to break. We should have focused on equipping them to find solutions to problems without 'running back' to the organisation. A 'dependency syndrome' set in, which was compounded by the sense of identity and belonging these particular boys had with the project and its facilities. Staff were abused verbally and told by the lads that if it wasn't for them they would not be in employment. They made increasingly elaborate demands and were at times manipulative, playing one staff member off against another. They would dominate and use several hours of staff time in getting disputes settled. It was hard at the time to measure the negative impact on the rest of the project. On reflection we realised that the age group below the dominant group had been neglected. When behaviour became aggressive and younger children were targeted, stones thrown at buildings and threats to staff and property took on a more serious level than before we were forced to act. The fear amongst staff, who were well used to danger and difficult circumstances personally and professionally, was far greater than I had appreciated. At a meeting held in secret, five senior members of staff shared how some older lads had threatened to poison not just them but their families too.

Important lessons needed to be learned. We needed to understand challenging and disturbing behaviour and not take it personally. We needed to learn that by instilling fears in others, the lads were projecting their own fears and insecurities. We needed to learn afresh the 'art' of social work – to befriend in order to make professional judgement rather than seeking friendship. We needed to revisit the issues of identity and ownership and change our language accordingly. We needed to get serious about boundaries and exit strategies for each lad to ensure a sustainable and happy outcome for them as young adults in a wider society to which they belonged. In short – we had to recommit to and strengthen a *transitional approach.*

To conclude, we met several times with the group as a whole and then agreed with them that each of them had different history, personality and needs, experience of the project to date and aspirations. We identified and worked with natural, smaller alliances within the larger group to design a plan for each individual. We then spent a year systematically preparing individuals for 'graduation' from the project. Of course there were the usual struggles, unexpected events, false starts and external threats but the focus had changed. Graduations became more ceremonial and all lads were invited to applaud effort and witness certificates, tools and equipment being given to the graduate as a final send-off. There would still be occasional visits but this event marked the end of the 'transition' to a new destination. Highlighting these events, referencing them in our language and keeping the concepts of journey and movement alive in our everyday thinking ensured the implications of a transitional approach were understood and accepted.

Summary

In Chapter 3 two processes were examined: entering the world of street children and engaging with street children. These processes manifest a relational approach and in our situation were reflected in street work, medical work, sports and feeding programmes.

The five components that follow in the appendices to this ahapter are shown in the diagram on page 15 and were designed to ensure a transitional approach:

1. the drop in centre
2. transitional education
3. transitional residential care
4. reconciliation and reunification with relatives
5. integration into existing families

Of course the transition of children through the programme was rarely smooth and there would be false starts, detours, disappointments and unexpected events all the time. The journey is far more likely to resemble a rocky or African 'murram' road than smooth tarmac!

Appendix 1. The drop in centre (The Tigers Clubhouse)
History and background

Even before arriving in Uganda we envisaged some kind of drop in centre and knew that street child programmes often included such a facility. However, it was good that resources did *not* allow us to build, buy or rent one immediately. With resources it is too tempting – and in some contexts too easy – to rush into what sounds like a good plan without careful preparation and consideration about what is actually needed.

For over a year we had no premises. Street work, feeding, counselling and administration were carried out in a Land Rover or from the back of a jeep. With hindsight it was a good thing; it prevented hiding behind structures and programmes, it enabled the organisation to grow organically and become established both legally and practically and it allowed time to raise funds so that we knew there was enough to complete each phase of development before we began. Most importantly, it meant street work and being on the move around the city ensured the processes of entering the world of street children and street children engaging with us were really happening.

From 1996 to early 1998 we were given the use of a small room in a technical college in one of Kampala's biggest slums. At the time, we were thrilled to have something even though not much bigger than a cupboard in which everything happened – lessons, team meetings, counselling, medical work, administration, accounts and storage of all equipment. Outreach through sports, medical and street work continued so it became a base from which people came and went throughout the day.

An extraordinary series of events enabled us to buy a centre that I had noticed not long after arriving in Uganda. I commented at the time how brilliant it would be to own it one day and it was worth the wait. The location and size were ideal for us. It was between two slum areas heavily populated with street children, many who we already knew, and comprised of two buildings (one brick, the other wooden), garages and storage area and a courtyard. Work began the day we purchased it to build a secure perimeter wall, to knock down and reconstruct the wooden building, to build washing facilities and additional toilets, to put in a cooking area with wood stoves and to fix roofing and ceiling boards. The place was decorated and furnished over the next 12 months. In keeping with the sports focus in our outreach, it was called The Clubhouse and opened officially by the King of Buganda, Kabaka Ronald Mutebi II.

That was an extremely significant day I will never forget – for many reasons. Although we had built a friendship with the Kabaka and had historic family links, entertaining royalty proved to be a steep learning curve. Minutes before the scheduled arrival, security came and found we had failed to spread grass mats on areas of the plot not yet covered with tarmac. The monarch was not supposed to tread directly on the ground so I jumped in the van with three lads and a frantic search for the right quantity and type of mats began. I knew that in Ugandan culture it is accepted the more important you are the later you can be. However I politely urged the

Kabaka's private secretary to encourage him to arrive in reasonable time. It was a shock when the entourage arrived only minutes late and I had to change clothes after my mat-finding venture. Thankfully, others stepped in to welcome the Kabaka on arrival and I managed to pull my trousers on before rushing out to the courtyard! A fabulous ceremony followed but the most poignant moment came at the opening itself. In fact it became a defining moment for the organisation as a whole as it captured the very essence of all we would stand for. It was the moment a king and a street child held a pair of scissors together – hand in hand – in order to cut the tape and announce our humble drop in centre officially open. The media loved it and published numerous photos on front pages. It was like an enactment of prophetic verses found in the Bible in Psalm 113 which state, 'He sits the poor with the princes of their people' and challenged us to uphold the value and inherent worth of every child we were to work with.

That is the background to establishing a drop in centre in Kampala unlike any we had come across and probably the first of its kind. The background story in Addis Ababa differs but in a similar way relationship building, understanding the context and establishing our identity happened *prior* to the drop in centre being opened.

Defining purpose and objectives

Before designing a programme or implementing activities, specific objectives of a drop in centre should be defined. A diligent board of trustees or directors may wonder whether the organisation actually needs a drop in centre. They might ask, 'Can't we achieve these objectives in a more cost-effective way?' or 'Why can't street work itself prepare a child for transition into the community?' I argued that in the contexts we worked, there were limitations and constraints to working directly with children on the street. The journey children needed to make in order to enter or reintegrate into mainstream community life required stability, strength and support which could best be offered and found at a location near but not actually 'on' the street.

The general purpose of a transitional approach has been stated and all elements, including a drop in centre, should be designed and relate to each other in order to fulfil it. Examples of specific objectives of a drop in centre may include:

- To create an environment within which a street child feels able to tell their story, share information, express their feelings and make informed choices regarding their future.
- To provide facilities and resources to address urgent needs and issues that may hinder a child's development and growth or undermine their rights.
- To be a safe haven and secure premises in order to protect especially vulnerable children and young people and remove them from harm.
- To enable children and young people to access recreational and educational opportunities that will empower them to make informed choices.

In each example I have tried to relate the place or programme to the process of a child transitioning from one place or state to another. The drop in centre can serve as a bridge in many ways; linking befriending on the street to deeper relationships, linking basic welfare services dealing with immediate needs to those concerned with longer term or deeper needs, linking fear and responses to trauma to growing security and self-worth, linking initial curiosity in the project to raised expectations and interest in alternatives to the street. There are many more 'bridges' on each particular child's journey that need to be crossed and will be if a drop in centre is run effectively.

Emergency accommodation

The words 'drop in' imply openness, lack of formal programme and that appointments are not necessary to enter. The city centre clubhouse was intended as a daytime facility and has remained that way. However, we quickly recognised the need for emergency short-term accommodation and in response allowed one area of the centre to be a 'refuge' for especially vulnerable children. The criteria for allowing a child to enter were:

- To ensure ongoing medical treatment in serious cases.
- To complete a period of preparation immediately prior to resettlement (this criteria was set before the opening of the halfway home).
- To provide a place of safety for a particularly young or vulnerable child.

It was hard to limit space to children within these criteria. All staff members and children needed a clear understanding of why the refuge existed. It was not a 'night shelter' for any street child. I knew dozens of shelters which had been allowed to deteriorate in standards and staffing and ended up simply being an extension to street life.

At the clubhouse, facilities were basic and bedding was not evident during the day. Mattresses and blankets were pulled out in the evening and put away the following morning. In this way the message was given that the refuge was not a 'destination' itself – it was a temporary, emergency, stop-gap arrangement for those with particular needs or circumstances. The process of finding a permanent alternative to the street was our priority. It took some staff a while to fully appreciate that running a fixed night shelter could hinder that process and lead to compromising aims and outcomes.

Creating a conducive environment

Creating the right environment at a drop in centre takes time. The environment or ambience can be cultivated but cannot be artificially manufactured. It needs to develop as the project grows and learns from experience. Each centre is unique and although it is helpful to visit others and to reference what others have learned, no two centres are the same. However, to be an environment conducive to social work relationships and effective interventions, every drop in centre should be:

- *Open* – both in terms of the 'front gate' and within the premises. Not every drop in centre can or should have a totally open door policy. In Uganda, the Clubhouse was open on most days for any street child to walk in through the gates unless there was a specific reason why the guard should not allow them in. Activities and staff availability varied but those simply needing space away from the street, to wash themselves or their clothes or to meet with other street children still came in and out freely. After dark – which in East Africa is always within minutes of seven o'clock – entry was restricted to specific children or by prior arrangement with a staff team member. In Ethiopia, the numbers of children, capacity and location of the drop in centre and stage of project development all contributed to a decision to control use of the drop in centre. Two or three times a year, the team decided which street children would be allowed access. It depended on the circumstances, information gathered on the street and apparent readiness to move away from street life. The premises itself and the environment both 'communicate' to street children the ethos and values of the project. I came across a disturbing example of a drop in centre that seemed to reinforce the view that street children were not worth bothering about. Basic facilities can suffice but in this instance they had not been cared for, litter and waste were everywhere and pit latrines were in a bad way. There was evidence of glue sniffing and cannabis, posters were torn, and there were no books or equipment. Staff presence was minimal and volunteers came to prepare food most days. Lack of resources could have been blamed but the same organisation had a separate administrative centre about half a mile away. It was comfortable, well furnished and populated by senior staff members reading newspapers – perpetually in some cases. You may be unlikely to risk adopting such a two-tier approach which gives damaging messages to children who may already believe they are worthless. However, there is still a danger of sliding into less overtly unfair arrangements. Drop in centres can be noisy, smelly and crowded – conducive to good social work but not to administration, accounts or report writing. For a long time we managed to keep all departments in the same location (at the Clubhouse) until it was no longer manageable. A modest office was found for accounts and administration but to assure children they had not been abandoned by staff members for more comfortable surroundings, some offices remained and staff meetings still occurred at the drop in centre. It needed to be seen as a good place for both staff and lads to hang out. The level of activity varied but we aspired for staff to be present and the place to be alive and busy most of the time to prevent lethargy and carelessness setting in.

- *Secure* – the internal and external contexts of a drop in centre determine levels of security needed to create an environment that enables good social work to happen. In Uganda and more specifically the area that the drop in centre was located, a guard was necessary – for a season both day and night. Employing security staff was normal and when we had to 'upgrade' to a trained and licensed armed guard, from one with a bow and arrow, it was entirely appropriate considering the nature and level of crime in that area and some specific threats. It was the job of the warden to ensure the guard's presence was a positive one – allowing children inside to feel safe and free to enjoy themselves. Induction was essential so the guard understood our ethos, aims and priorities. At times, guards had to be replaced for colluding with older lads or other lapses in responsibility but the system was appropriate for the context and worked well most of the time.

- *Safe* – this is related to but broader than security issues discussed above. Child safeguarding or child protection is of paramount importance in all areas and must be included in designing, planning and running drop in centres. Some examples of safety measures developed were:
  - Visitors policy which determined who was allowed in, when and for what reasons; this included friends and relatives of staff team members. The wider child protection policy ensured that all visitors or volunteers had to be checked by CRB (Criminal Record Bureau) or equivalent if available. If that wasn't possible personal or written references were sought and visitors accompanied at all times.
  - A code of conduct, which was the section of a Child Protection Policy, was laminated and displayed in offices and central areas. It reminded staff and children of expectations and ways to protect themselves and others from misunderstanding or abusive behaviour.
  - Use of images policy which included procedures before any photos were taken and agreements about the use of images, quotations and information outside the drop in or other project premises.
  - Care of property. A drop in centre – in sharp contrast to the street – should be safe at every level. Risks need to be identified and managed in relation to the condition of the property, power and water supplies. A system of cleaning not only enhances pride in centre users but can prevent accidents and illness. It was easier to say than do as we discovered when introducing coloured bins for the site and attempting to motivate lads to use them!

- *Child-friendly* – in any context there are ways of transforming stark and unwelcoming buildings to places where children immediately feel relaxed and accepted. It is worth repeating that premises themselves communicate to children something about their worth and the extent to which the place exists for them. In Johannesburg an entire hospital complex was handed to child-related agencies of all kinds. I was amazed at how from the moment you walked in it was obvious that this was a place 'for' children – the brightly coloured corridors, clear signs, vibrant posters all contributed to this effect. With agencies dealing with everything from phobias of dentists to training for court appearances in child abuse cases the opposite could so easily have been true. In Kampala, the perimeter wall, gates and inside walls were decorated in lively colours and an artist from the UK trained boys to create the most incredible murals capturing the mood and environment we hoped for at the centre.

Designing a flexible programme

The main activities at the drop in centre are listed below and many existing organisations describe similar programmes in their literature. In our context there needed to be structured activity to offer routine and opportunity to build relationship and understanding but flexibility to ensure we could respond in creative ways to each child:

Play – Those who work on rubbish dumping grounds or at least witness them on documentaries notice that even in those places children play. It is fundamental that every child grows and learns through play. There is something liberating about pure laughter that comes through and from play and something equally distressing about children who are denied the opportunity to play on a daily basis. Such denial grates as play is a natural and intrinsic part of human development. Even with limited resources, play should be at the heart of a drop in centre. In our case we made and painted brightly coloured giant board games (including Ludo, a national favourite in Uganda), table tennis, balls to play with and organised team games and races at various times. At later stages of the programme play was used in a therapeutic way in social work intervention. There are foundations and organisations such as Play Therapy International or Right To Play that provide examples, guidance, training and resources to develop this.

Food – The feeding programme was 'open' on some days which meant that any child who was living on the street could come and receive hot food. The context meant it was not an unconditional handout. Normally beans, tomatoes, rice or maize meal ('posho'), cabbage and pineapple were served to around 200 children. Staff and older lads in the 'Junior Management Team' looked out for new or recent arrivals and tried to gather information or check details for consistency. Before and after the meal news and information were shared with the group as a whole and responses or ideas heard. In the early years we combined this with simple life skills lessons, guidance on certain issues or encouragement aimed particularly at those we only saw once or twice a week. Some staff used a story from their experience or from the Bible to illustrate points being made. The open feeding was, however, exactly that and there were no demands put on children or strings attached – all were treated equally and with respect.

Health – Some details of the medical work are given in Chapter 2. As the drop in centre developed the capacity and services of the medical team grew. At certain times the clinic – staffed by a full time nurse and health team volunteers – had an open door policy. At other times it was restricted to on-going treatment and dressing of wounds or the staff were escorting or visiting children in hospital or at a local surgery. The medical team reported that some children primarily sought attention and wanted to be heard. Some were initially more willing to go to the nurse than to a social worker, so gathering and sharing information with relevant members of the team was essential.

Hygiene – Play, nutrition, medical care and a broader emphasis on hygiene all address street children's physical needs and tangibly demonstrate concern for their most basic needs. Physical growth and health, improvements in appearance, hair and skin condition, increased energy and stamina indicated positive self-esteem and resilience. That was why we prioritised building a washing block and providing areas and equipment for cleaning and drying clothes. In a setting either hot and dusty or hot and muddy it was never easy to keep the premises clean but doing so cultivated a sense of pride and responsibility and set an example for the future.

Education – The Clubhouse included a 'Learning Centre' which was open to all those who came regularly to the drop in centre. Street children invariably cite education as their number one desire. This may be sincere and accurate or it could be a learned response to those offering help. It is what people seeking to help want to hear and long-term street children are often aware of that. Providing education at a drop in centre enables a child to know whether it really is something they want and at the same time enables the project to measure commitment and assess levels of education. The team discovered early on that one of the greatest challenges was handling a wide range of educational ability with little space, few staff and limited resources. Having visited and met street child agencies in other countries this seems to be a universal problem. Curriculum design, lesson plans, classroom layout, materials and techniques need to reflect a desire to meet these challenges. The education programme is described in more detail below although it is not possible to cover every aspect. Resources and advice are available for those educating children still on the street from organisations such as *JUCONI* in Mexico, *OASIS Global, CSC, Street Kids International* or *Open Schools Worldwide* which developed an inspiring programme in South Africa:

> The 'school-in-a-bag' contains a specially written literacy and mathematics course called 'Count Me In', character development, life skills and health education materials, a Bible-based counselling programme and all the necessary stationery and teaching resources. The course is called 'Count Me In' to reflect that God loves these children that society has rejected, abused and neglected . . . Attendance is free and classes operate at times and places convenient for the children they serve.

www.openschoolsworldwide.org

Titus was a 16 year old who had never held a pencil before and needed to learn fine motor skills to control one. Almost without exception the street children we met had missed out on formal education or like Titus, had never been to school. Age was no indicator of educational level reached. The morale of older teenagers, who had not experienced 'baby class,' as it was called in Uganda, was easily diminished and motivating them to learn was hard. The project was respected amongst its peers for working with what were known as 'hard-core' street youth. For some of them, gaps in formal education were too great and other options such as vocational training or starting a business were explored.

For those who responded positively and were motivated, rapid improvement was sometimes noted. Titus went on to read and write in both Luganda and English to a standard he was able to enter vocational training. Younger children were able to enter or re-enter mainstream school having caught up to a reasonable level but just as importantly having learned to attend, focus and interact with fellow pupils and those in authority.

Managing risks and facing challenges

Running a drop in centre is never easy. By definition it is a free and open meeting place between those on the street and members of the organisation or project. There will be challenges, confrontation and even conflict as two 'worlds' interrelate. Handling this is a learned skill, closely linked to creating an environment for effective social work. It became the focus of regular staff meetings and staff team development days as we sought ways to improve skills and increase support for each other:

Discipline

As a positive environment emerged there was a need to find ways of encouraging cooperation and healthy dynamics as well as deterring children from behaviour that was a threat to themselves or others. A natural extension of the discipline needed for football training and matches to succeed came in the form of red cards and yellow cards at the drop in centre. We used language already familiar to the members to emphasise that just as a football team needs structures and boundaries to function (and win) so too did the community at the drop in centre if it was to achieve its goals. As on the pitch a yellow card was issued as a warning. After receiving two yellow cards a red card would be issued which would lead to some form of penalty. The boys themselves designed a chart of offences that deserved a yellow card and those that may lead to an immediate red card. They enjoyed this process and were acutely aware of what behaviours should be on the chart. A red card usually meant a suspension from the programme for a specified period. We rarely had to enforce it because of the stigma that came with it. If a boy got several red cards it would lead to other restrictions and on three occasions we had to make the painful decision to disallow a child to return. In each case the tipping point came when his presence hindered the work of the project or when the response to multiple opportunities was continually negative. There were a few times when an organisation we were in partnership with was contacted and we were able to explain the situation and refer the child on. Rather than seeing this as 'passing the buck' it was an acknowledgement that no one organisation can meet the needs of every child. Another project may have an approach or activities that, for whatever reason, are more appropriate for a particular child. The process was reciprocal and at times we would give children who had been referred to us by other organisations a fresh opportunity.

The rules of the centre were stated in positive language and wording. Eye-catching posters were designed by the lads themselves and placed in each building. Rather than listing what they were not allowed to do, they tied results with promoting positive or avoiding negative behaviour, for example:

At Tigers Club:
- We respect each other's property so *we do not steal.*
- We discuss and solve problems so *we do not fight.*
- We want to be strong and healthy so *we do not smoke or take drugs.*
- We enjoy being at the clubhouse so *we do not damage windows or property.*

Confrontation and conflict

Both words are strong and imply hostility, clashes and even prolonged battle but there are times when working with street children on a daily basis feels exactly like that! Handling challenging behaviour is a crucial skill in running a drop in centre which is why we devoted time to it in staff team development. This section refers to the most common incidents or behaviours which were *dysphoric* – fuelled or driven by emotion. It would be a strange or rare street child project that did not encounter dysphoric behaviour on a regular basis. Difficult behaviour caused or driven by a disturbed mind may be *psychotic* or even *psychopathic* and dealing with it is more rare and beyond the scope of this particular book.

Dysphoric, emotion driven behaviour may take the form of rage against staff team members or other street children or fighting as we experienced often in the early years at the drop in centre. These occasions tend to happen very quickly and we all react instinctively 'in the heat of the moment'. If the threat is extreme or acute our bodies respond in a sequence psychologists describe as 'freeze, flight or fight'. We become hyper-vigilant or alert and freeze in a way that is often associated with fear, we look for a way to flee and if that fails we attempt to fight. The thinking part of the brain is superceded or bypassed so that the area responsible for these responses can 'instruct' the body directly. This is important information. When tempers flare or a fight breaks out in front of us our behaviour may seem beyond our control. However, if we are aware of these responses and how the body functions we can add techniques for handling explosive times. In a sense we supplement what the body does naturally.

As a team we reviewed some incidents, tried to analyse how we responded and came up with the following:

- One team member spoke of times when one of the lads had 'pressed the wrong button at the wrong time'. We all understood exactly what he meant and *identified triggers*.
- Blood pressure and temperatures rise and heart beat increases which correspond to the *automatic responses* mentioned above.
- One of the most important things at this stage is to *depersonalise any confrontation and our response*. There will be moments, those split seconds, when we are able to think and a pre-prepared message to ourselves should be 'This anger or rage is *not* about me. There are other issues and reasons for it even if it seems to be directed at me.'
- The time to raise those issues is not at this point but verbalising that you know the child is feeling angry or that something has upset them may create more momentary pauses for reflection. Do not judge the anger but *demonstrate that you understand* it.
- The priority must then be to *restore safety*.
- *Repetition* may be relevant to defuse the situation. A calm but strong presence should be reflected in the voice with repeated instructions to 'sit down', 'back away', or 'move over here (to another area)'. The tasks should be clear and simple and offer further opportunity to redirect or channel energy.

Many street children fight to survive and protect themselves but also have a deep sense of justice. It was fascinating to see how in the midst of a fight lads would express outrage at perceived mistreatment or lack of fairness. Stolen or damaged property was often the key issue or at least trigger. In order to create safety lads were separated and conceded to repeated commands which aimed to shift the desire for victory to a desire for resolution.

When a fight or rage seems to be subsiding it is important to remember the situation is still volatile. Without making promises that will be impossible to keep, language should be used to emphasise that it is a shared problem and that the solution will be shared. 'We know you are upset; we understand why you are feeling angry; we will work at this together' are all key messages at this stage. Further possible responses to conflict and confrontation to consider include:

'Tactical ignoring' – A strategy to use when challenging or disturbing behaviour is driven by the desire for attention. It can be used in sophisticated behaviour change management programmes, everyday parenting or work with street children in drop in centres. The staff team in Uganda imagined and re-enacted several scenarios that had occurred or could occur at the drop in centre. In some cases it seemed best to ignore behaviour with the following conditions:

- We were certain the behaviour was designed to get attention. Social workers or other team members had to tune into the particular child and make a quick analysis of behaviour.
- A message was given that non-aggressive and appropriate behaviour would lead to the right sort of attention and response. This is known as *positive reinforcement*.

Working as a team – In the same way individuals reveal their true nature under stress, teams expose how well they are working when in dangerous situations or under stress. It is vital that teams are strengthened *before* such challenges arise so again the need for team building and strong support must be emphasised – they are not optional 'add-ons' within a social work context. I believe that leaders who delegate responsibility to care for children or young people in difficult circumstances to others have a moral obligation to provide team and individual support and supervision. It is a legal requirement in some countries. In relation to handling conflict and confrontation, team members need to share their own experience, fears and concerns. By being open – in a safe environment – others will be able to offer the kind and level of support needed during and after difficult incidents. Leaders are not exempt from these demands or needs.

On one occasion I was collecting equipment from the drop in centre for staff training being held elsewhere. Two older boys, Salim and Godfrey, banged on the gate repeatedly and demanded to be let in. As I was reversing my vehicle out, they appeared from behind the perimeter wall and entered. The security guard warned them and in response the lads pulled out knives. With added pressures of hosting project visitors and having to get to the training session, I 'resolved' this conflict with some knee-jerk reactions, a lot of shouting and probably more 'fight' than 'flight' response than was needed. It was a happy coincidence that the training was happening because we were able to de-brief during the initial session. The team offered support, discussed the incident, steps needed to be taken and strategies for the future.

Knowing when to support another worker is important and this is often down to staff being ruthlessly honest about how they are coping. If we sense that intervention is needed or that we need to withdraw as we are struggling to retain a rational approach, it is imperative to say so or give signals to make it clear.

On another occasion I had been on the receiving end of a barrage of complaints and finger-wagging (derogatory in that context). I withdrew by driving aimlessly for a long time, parking at the top of Kampala's only multi-storey car park and weeping uncontrollably. The lad involved had been the focus of our attention for months and it seemed our endeavours counted for nothing. In fact, his anger was related to wider issues so I needed to depersonalise the messages, seek and find support from other team members and defuse the situation.

Public relations

If a drop in centre is going to strategically enable an organisation to fulfil its vision, it is likely to be located in an area well known to street children. It is likely to be in a densely populated area and congruent with the surrounding environment. Those features mean it will be exposed to neighbours and the wider community and those running it need to be prepared for the challenge of public relations. We have already discussed public attitudes to street children which are sometimes informed and fuelled by negative images in the media. People believe and assume certain things about street children so a place that gathers them will attract attention. That was most evident when street and former street children at the drop in centre were continually blamed for things that went wrong in the area – damage to property, noise at night, thefts and attacks on people or cars. The role of the Clubhouse Warden was critical in building strong relations with the community and that meant being proactive rather than simply reacting to complaints or events. The community included neighbours, traders, police and local defence units as well as religious and council leaders. 'Open Days' were held to inform and inspire individuals from those groups. We included formal presentations, question and answer sessions, lads giving their testimonies, displays and time for networking and informal discussion over refreshments. In addition, visits were made to local groups, the chairman's office, police post, schools and homes in order to explain the work, foster good relations and ensure lines of communication were open. Whenever there was a wave of violent crime, car-jacking or theft, staff and the boys themselves were no longer assumed to be the source of the problem but able to participate in response to it.

Summary

This section has highlighted the value of a drop in centre as one component of a transitional approach. To be effective and to offer clarity to street children themselves, the wider community, donors and authorities the specific purpose and objectives of a drop in centre should be defined and articulated. The nature of services provided, the programme at the drop-in centre and the environment created all contribute to ensuring it is genuinely transitional – one part of a journey. We considered three fundamental processes: creating a conducive environment which is open, secure, safe and child-friendly; designing a flexible programme which in our example entailed play, food, health care provision and education; managing risks and facing challenges including discipline, confrontation and conflict. Drop-in centres are likely to be in areas close to where street children spend the majority of their time for example near bus or train stations, close to markets or densely populated slum areas. As such those that operate them need to handle public relations with great care and a brief description of what that entailed was given.

Appendix 2. Transitional education (The Learning Centre)

We have considered education in the context of the drop in centre where the Learning Centre was a core setting for assessment and relationship building. The issues of motivation and handling multiple abilities in a resource-constrained environment were raised and the inherent value and purpose of education in addition to its function as a stepping-stone to reintegration into mainstream schooling were highlighted.

I am indebted to those who were directly involved in teaching street and former street children for their contribution to this section. They shared experiences and lessons learned at the grassroots level and these are incorporated below.

Purpose

The overall purpose of education which aims to be transitional include:

- To assist street children to re-enter mainstream schooling at a reasonable level for their age.
- To enable children to move from chaos to routine in order to cope with the demands of formal education.
- To engage street children in the learning process and develop skills and self-esteem.

Teaching staff identified aims that were more immediately achievable and reflected more elemental needs and concerns.

> *I was aiming . . . for children to push through the barrier of beginning to read. Without this they really struggled to access anything that was being offered to them at the Learning Centre or later in school.*

> *Not being in class knocks a child's confidence. Rebuilding confidence is key to reintegration into school. Other aims included life skills such as routine, discipline and time-keeping as well as social skills in sharing, ability to discuss, manners, teamwork and responding positively to authority.*

The context was Global. Whatever the context, purposes of transitional education must relate to the expectations, style of teaching and educational practices that a child may encounter in mainstream education.

Planning

The education programme had to be designed in a way that was appropriate for the purpose of reintegration. Our planning sought to ensure cohesion in children's learning and continuity between what was taught at the learning centre and what would be covered in school. For those working cross-culturally it is essential to have some idea of how children are taught in local schools. A programme resembling mainstream school has to be balanced with the need for accelerated learning in order to enable children to enter school at an appropriate level. One teacher wrote in relation to this balance:

> The resource from Oasis Uganda was fantastic for reading skills: a fast way to teach children to read. The children loved the interaction and being taught in small groups of six or eight. However, the teaching methods were very different to those in Ugandan schools. We took the national curriculum for English, pulled out the key objectives and used these at each level.

Classrooms were laid out in a similar way to those in Ugandan schools with children sat in rows. However, in recognition of the need for affirmation, work done was displayed and celebrated. Lesson plans were kept simple and workable with scope for flexibility and postponing some learning points until the following lesson. In mixed groups questions and activities were set according to level of ability.

Teachers discovered a lower than expected attention span among street children and consequently tailor made the timetable so that time in class could be increased steadily. Frequent breaks were scheduled in especially for new arrivals at the Learning Centre. At the halfway home the timetable followed the hours and times of mainstream schools and attendance and punctuality became increasingly important in the weeks prior to a boy leaving.

Business skills training

For some older boys entering or returning to mainstream school was not feasible. Some were enabled to start micro-enterprises and it quickly became apparent that extra training was needed in general business skills, irrespective of the enterprise being launched. A basic curriculum was developed covering planning, bookkeeping, budgeting, marketing and presentation, handling customers and integrity in the workplace. For some, completing the course was a prerequisite to securing a start-up grant. Street Kids International has expertise in this area and is listed as a possible source of information and support.

Staffing

It was critical to find staff not only qualified to teach but who demonstrated certain other qualities. Enthusiasm, patience, approachability and excellence in handling challenging behaviour are necessary to deal with added demands of children who have experienced traumatic events prior to and while living on the street:

> We needed enthusiastic teachers who were willing to learn, organised and inspired enough to make the most of the time allotted to classroom teaching.

A child's portfolio of work was shared with their new school. After enrolling and starting at school, contact continued with regular visits to provide continuity and track progress being made.

Appendix 3. Transitional residential care (The Halfway Home – Tudabujja)

Vision and purpose

Nine miles from Uganda's capital city is a place devoted to renewal, restoration and hope. From the main tarmac road linking Kampala and Entebbe airport, it is a 20 minute drive on mud road towards the shores of Lake Victoria. The space it occupies was 10 acres of wild and overgrown bush and the 11 month process to own it was long, arduous and at times hazardous. The faith, sacrifice and effort that went into the development of this part of the work were greater than all the other parts combined. There were times when it would have been easier to give up on this venture and continue as before. So, why did it mean so much? What value would be added to the work by having such a facility?

The short answer was captured by older lads who entered a competition to find a name for the centre. We explained the vision as best we could and then left them to it. The winner suggested adapting the word usually applied to furniture restoration – bidabujja. He described this as making a piece of furniture look like it did when it was first made. By replacing 'bi-' with 'tu-' it was personalised to mean 'we are being made new'. 'Tudabujja' meant being restored to what was intended. Tudabujja was to be a place where in-depth work would equip and empower children with skills and strength to thrive in family and community.

Of course we had resettled children to their villages prior to opening Tudabujja and had even facilitated some foster care placements but we were concerned to offer the best we could. The aim was to increase the chances of children not just remaining in their villages but thriving, contributing to the life of the family and influencing others with all they had learned and become. Qualitative outcomes are as important as quantitative ones unless we are content with a 'sticky-plaster' remedy or surface response to the problems faced by street children. Tudabujja was a facility to add quality to our response.

Many people ask about our experience of buying land or property in Africa. The relatively low costs of land and construction appeal to those who want to 'do something' – it is tangible and can sometimes be done quickly. One aid agency urged us to pause before doing so and to focus on building human capacity rather than bricks and mortar. It was valuable advice and for three years we focussed on strengthening a national staff team and establishing relationships with street children before embarking on buying land. With hindsight we are grateful that resources dictated the order of events and prevented us doing otherwise. It was crucial to have a strong presence on the street and in the city *before* developing Tudabujja. The 'cutting edge' of our work depended on the city centre site being viewed as the heart or 'hub' by both staff team members and street children – from which children would then continue their journey.

Location and layout

Location was important and we limited our search for land was limited to plots within a 20 mile radius. The reasons for this related to both children and organisation. Street children were in transition and the destination was often a rural area and all that involved. It was important to introduce or reintroduce children to the rhythm and demands of rural life whilst acknowledging the reality of urban migration. Many had been city-dwellers and could be in the future so it was important to equip them for that possibility too. The land we chose, out of 14 possibilities, was on the outskirts of the capital but had a rural feel not unlike the areas many residents would return to or share with their new foster families.

Before deciding to buy, specialists in agriculture and livestock were invited and their guidance led to a 'dream layout design' for the entire site. They advised us about what to grow and where, irrigation and accessing water, areas suitable for residential development and how to use the land to maximise its potential.

Learning from others

While construction was underway, the Board approved a proposal to visit nine residential facilities for street children in three South African cities. It was extremely worthwhile to assess feasibility and glean from others what they had learned from their experiences. I wanted to explore criteria and selection for admission, how centres related to those working on the streets or to authorities, programmes within the centres, the environment, length of stay and destinations of residents, discipline issues, other challenges and to get a feel for each centre's regime. General information learned and specific insights gained contributed to our planning but it was important to remember we were embarking on something unique. No two centres are the same and we resolved to learn from others but also stick to what was right for our particular context and to achieve our particular aims.

Design fit for purpose

The design tried to reflect the purposes outlined above. The residential area comprised four small homes on the perimeter of a grassy circle. Each home accommodated eight children in two rooms and a residential care worker in an inter-linked room. They were simple in design but built with materials intended to last. Each home had an outside kitchen area and space for a small 'shamba' or garden for fruit and vegetables. In the centre of the circle we built a large banda – a thatched, circular hut – which was large enough for the whole community to meet for meals, games, lessons and other gatherings. It stood as a symbol of community and it was a privilege to witness occasions of celebration as well as urgent meetings to resolve conflict.

Other buildings included two homes for the centre manager and a farm manager with space for families if necessary, a four-room 'gatehouse' for stores and security staff and farm buildings including accommodation for older lads training as farm apprentices.

Around 60 per cent of the land was developed for cultivation and livestock and the flattest area was – after considerable grading and levelling – designated for football and other sports. We included changing areas to enable visiting teams and a covered area for spectators.

The design and layout reflected the vision for children to prepare for and experience: home and family life, health and recreation, education, training and self-sustainable agriculture which remains the most fundamental means of livelihood for the majority of the population.

Attitude or mindset

As with other areas, people warned us the halfway home concept wouldn't work. I am grateful to sceptics because their doubts sometimes stir a greater determination to prove something can and **will** work. Of course there were times when the centre or programme didn't fulfil the vision it was designed for or meet expectations as capably as hoped. Critical review and reflection was necessary to find reasons and deal with issues rather than abandoning or compromising the vision for transformation and transition into the community.

Residential care in East Africa is often assumed to be long-term. Whether in the form of boarding schools for the elite or orphanages for those assumed to be without family, the prevailing view is that once accepted or admitted a child will remain there for a long period of time. The staff team decided that the length of stay at Tudabujja should be on average six months. That was felt to be a reasonable length of time to achieve the aims in mind unless there were exceptional circumstances. What happens – we were often asked – if children don't want to leave? How will you ensure children don't get stuck at Tudabujja?

The answers to those questions were almost always to do with attitude and perception. The concept of a halfway home must be understood within the context of a *transitional* approach. It is part of a journey. Although staff members knew this in theory, once they experienced the challenge and joy of witnessing children passing *through* the centre and *on* to something 'better' they began to grasp its significance. The attitude of residents was equally important. Before construction was near completion we introduced the idea of the halfway home as a place of preparation. We encouraged terminology which would mean children equated Tudabujja with movement and journey. It was a 'stepping stone' or 'springboard', the final stage or lap in a race. Before any child reached the halfway home he had to know where he was preparing to go to beyond his time there.

Residential care workers needed training and support to reinforce all that had been done prior to a child moving in. The number of children in each home resembled the numbers of children in homes throughout Uganda, the care worker may reflect a parental presence and the expectations within each house may parallel those in an ordinary family *but* it was not 'home' and care workers were not 'parents'. The emotional ties were never intended to grow as strong as those we hoped children would experience with their own relatives or foster families. A group mindset can alter as rapidly as an individual's so the team – at the drop in centre and halfway home – needed to constantly review their attitude and language in relation to Tudabujja to maintain the attitudes outlined.

Staffing

Most countries have guidelines, rules and legislation relating to residential care and it is important to be aware of and adhere to them. Child-to-staff ratio is usually included. As well as residential care workers, we allowed for field social workers to be present on a regular basis as well as a permanent teacher, centre manager and farm manager/trainer. On a typical day, that meant a four to one child to staff ratio decreasing to six-to-one at night. In addition, the project nurse made twice-weekly visits for check-ups and health education and other staff members came in on an ad hoc basis. Together they implemented the following programme.

Programme

The programme, which developed over the first two years of operations at Tudabujja, was designed to enable children to prepare practically, technically, emotionally, socially, spiritually and mentally for life with relatives or with a new family in the wider community. The content of each element was adapted to individual needs, maturity and ability as well as the expected length of stay at the centre:

- *Agricultural training* – The farm at Tudabujja was designed with training and demonstration in mind. It was never intended to be a commercial enterprise and even if it eventually became financially self-sustaining, its primary purpose of equipping children with skills needed to thrive in the community would remain. Our aim was to provide a broad training in cultivation and rearing livestock and then encourage residents to 'specialise' in particular areas according to their interests or the region they would soon be living in. Initially that entailed designating areas for staple crops such as cabbages, onions, tomatoes, matooke (green bananas), potatoes and maize. Another part of the farm was devoted to a piggery and cattle, rabbits and goats have also recently been introduced. A skilled agriculturalist was essential to manage the farm area effectively. All primary school children in Uganda study agricultural techniques so residents were taught the theory included in the national curriculum and practical skills.

  In other settings, street children may need different skills to sustain them in the future but in our situation the ability to 'dig the land' remains an essential skill for the majority of the population.

  Older boys who expressed an interest in agriculture were considered for an apprenticeship programme. Some lads knew they would inherit land and wanted to prepare for that eventuality, others knew they were more likely to be accepted in their villages of origin if they were skilled in certain aspects of farming and a third category were keen to be accepted by one of the agricultural training colleges with a view to commercial farming.

- *Education* – The vision for and implementation of a transitional education programme has been considered. At Tudabujja a purpose built learning centre was added to the initial development enabling teachers to provide meaningful lessons to a large number of children with varying abilities and interests. Residents were encouraged to view the learning centre as 'school' by wearing uniform and treating staff, their property and studies in the same way they would be expected to do so in the 'outside world'.
- *Domestic tasks and community living* – It was fascinating to hear from residential care workers about this aspect of the programme. Their task was to facilitate, encourage, support and monitor a journey from self-reliance and chaos to inter-dependence and routine. Recognising the strengths that so many street children have acquired through difficult circumstances was vital at the same time as keeping a realistic view on what needed to change or develop in order to increase the chances and quality of life beyond Tudabujja. Often, the way children learned to respond and relate to care workers improved in the first few months and would be mirrored later in relations with parents and grandparents. In Ugandan society there are norms and taboos that reflect inter-generational dynamics. It was critical that non-Ugandans developed a healthy respect for these dynamics and were diligent in hearing and understanding more about them from national staff.

  It is essential to be aware of what is the 'norm' in whatever setting you are based. Participation in duties around the home is a feature of life in many parts of Africa. Activities at Tudabujja therefore included: collecting water, preparing food, tidying and cleaning inside the home and the surrounding compound, digging the vegetable and fruit gardens, clearing and burning rubbish, participating in general cleaning, repairs and maintenance. Tasks were shared out fairly between staff and residents and rewards or incentives were given.
- *Recreation and sport* – Space was earmarked for sports and games – primarily for football but areas for volleyball and basketball too. Donors committed to providing or improving recreational facilities were relatively easy to find and one embassy funded the grading, levelling and planting of a full size football pitch as it corresponded exactly with their priority areas for funding. The inherent values of sport for physical fitness, team building and discipline are well documented.
- *Health education* – The project nurse and voluntary health assistants visited Tudabujja for regular clinics, emergencies, treatments and follow up. Their presence was always welcome. To be proactive in areas of health and hygiene, health education classes were incorporated into the programme. Together with a visiting football coach the nurse designed a 12 week course called '*How does Beckham keep so clean and healthy?*' It included games, exercises and activities to ensure that every resident covered key aspects of health and hygiene at least once during their stay at Tudabujja. HIV/AIDS prevention was constantly in our minds and placed within the broader context of sexual development, choices, relationships, respect for self and others, decision making, health and hygiene.
- *Social work* – Social workers who worked alongside children on the street and in the drop in centre continued to address key issues with individuals during their stay at Tudabujja. Working

in collaboration with residential staff, children were enabled to manage change and plan effectively for the next stage in their journey. Individual counselling and group work were reviewed in care meetings (called 'barazas' and described in Chapter 2). Areas addressed built on work done prior to entering the halfway home and included: continuing trauma-related issues, social skills and relationships, behavioural issues, anger, fear, self-esteem and dealing with authority.

- *Extra-curricular activities* – The programme included optional activities such as craft, drama, drumming and singing. The community gathered most evenings to share news and learn from each other. The project has a strong Christian foundation and ethos and for those who wanted, there were times to pray or read stories from the Bible.
- *Outings* – Occasionally visitors or staff team members arranged to take residents off site to experience something new. Outings were tied to significant or special events, to the education programme or 'graduation' of certain children from one stage of the process to another. Trips included the airport at Entebbe and the wildlife centre which had tailor made programmes for groups like ours.

Discipline

All residents at the halfway home had experienced life at the drop in centre and some had stayed at the emergency refuge. They were used to rules being expressed in positive language and the use of yellow cards and red cards to give a series of warnings before disciplinary measures. The discipline at Tudabujja used a system of incentives and rewards as well as withholding certain privileges such as outings.

Star charts

The boys themselves were asked to imagine how they would like their fellow residents to behave and treat others. They brainstormed a list of all the things that made someone a good example and from this exercise the first 'star chart' was designed. Participation in chores, cleanliness, respect for the care workers, being able to resolve differences were some areas included and each boy had the opportunity to gain gold stars for being exemplary and red stars for causing concern to the care worker. Once a specific number of gold stars were gained an award would be given and conversely some benefit withdrawn or privilege withheld if a specific number of red stars appeared. It was a simple but effective way of monitoring behaviour and measuring change.

Physical punishment

No two cultures are the same in the attitude toward and use of punishment. However, the culture of a residential centre should not necessarily emulate the society's prevailing attitudes to punishment. Why?

In our experience, many street children had been negatively impacted by methods of discipline and punishment which was manifest in their behaviour, developmental delays, difficulty in forming and sustaining relationships and beliefs about themselves. Using physical punishment in a residential centre runs the risk of adding further harm and evoking powerful memories. One early experience reinforced this thinking when two lads caught urinating on the side of one of the residential houses, were 'caned' by a new member of staff. It was a common enough sight in villages and schools to see children being threatened or even struck with a stick. Like many parts of Africa to strike with the hand was unacceptable. The staff member felt he had done the right thing and given a clear message. He told us, *'I just did what I would do to my own children'* assuming to do so was appropriate. That assumption had to be tackled immediately and an agreement with all staff reached that what they did at home was *not necessarily appropriate* at the halfway home. The children were not theirs, the setting and risks were not the same and non-physical alternatives had to be found.

Each context differs and in many parts of the world child safeguarding measures have been developed and refined over many years. In other places the concept of a 'child protection policy' is almost unheard of and terminology or definitions we take for granted are not yet in usage.

Leadership

Each component of a transitional approach demands strong and focussed leadership. Leaders need to fully understand how each component inter-relates and to ensure that it contributes to the fulfilment of an over-arching vision. The halfway home was no exception and leaders were expected to:

- Oversee the residential care and protection of all children living there. There are minimum standards in most countries and resources for those who are aiming for excellence in residential care. These are given at the end of this publication.
- Ensure that care plans were designed and implemented for each resident. This entailed working closely with social workers and having a clear view of why a child was there and for how long as well as the kind and extent of progress being made. This was the focus of the case conferences or barazas.
- Maintain the momentum of children entering and leaving the centre. We were weak at the outset in tracking the movement of children and measuring impact in this area. If an organisation is pioneering a new centre I encourage them to be far more diligent than we were about documenting facts and dates relating to each resident.
- Forge strong working relationships internally and with those implementing other aspects of the overall programme. Recruitment criteria had to include a commitment to team strengthening and building both within the halfway home team and the broader team. There is considerable risk of burnout amongst residential staff, which should determine priorities for staff care and supervision.

When these expectations are met a halfway home will be effective in realising its aims. The 'make or break' of a halfway home depends on adhering to admission criteria, children being prepared, entering, passing through and moving on to the next stage of their journey.

Summary

We have examined the purpose and process of developing a halfway home as one part of a transitional approach. It took time, effort, risks and sacrifice to make it happen but I hope the account given demonstrates that it is possible and inspires others. Mistakes were made and important lessons learned:

- Vision and purposes need to be defined and clearly articulated to explain what the halfway home is intended for; and equally what or who it is *not* for.
- The location and layout should be considered carefully to ensure they match the vision and purpose. For us, proximity to the capital and the work being done there was a key factor in decision-making.
- Being open to learn from others about core aspects and experiences of residential care is essential whilst remaining open to the possibility of creating something unique.
- Designs need to fit and relate to the agreed purposes.
- For the vision to be fulfilled it is essential to nurture the understanding and attitude of all involved. This is especially important when there are pre-conceived ideas about what is being planned.

The following four aspects of running a halfway home were described and some key issues or needs highlighted for consideration: *staffing, programme, discipline* and *leadership*.

Many visitors discover that there is something very special about Tudabujja. Actor James McAvoy visited in 2007 and reflected while he was there:

> *Everybody's incredibly honest that it's important for those being re-housed or given a foster family not just to be given a place to live but to be taught skills – agricultural skills, not just schooling and maths – but practical stuff to help them be useful members of society and attractive to prospective foster parents. That's incredible. It's an amazing place for a child to take respite – every child's been through something entirely personal.*

On The Tigers Trail Pt. 2 – Community Channel, 2007

A halfway home should be a great place at the same time as being a stepping-stone to a better one.

Appendix 4. Reconciliation and reunification with relatives (The Resettlement Programme)

Current thinking

Wherever there are large numbers of street children there are visions and schemes to reduce that number fuelled by a range of beliefs and motives. The police may have a vision to reduce the number of street children based on a belief that it will lead to a decrease in criminal activity.

City council departments may have a vision for a city with no street children motivated by a desire to assure the public they are being effective and so win votes. When I led a forum for street child agencies we received a directive from the Ministry of Tourism who had a vision for no street children. They believed tourists were being put off coming to the capital by the presence of street children. NGOs working with street children may be on the receiving end of pressure from these and other quarters to get the number of street children down – and to do so quickly! When dignitaries are coming to town or a city is hosting a regional or global conference, 'quickly' may mean immediately. I will never forget driving to the centre one morning and hearing on the radio news that 478 street children and youth had been removed from the street the night before in preparation for an American President's visit. That news altered our activity for the next three weeks and inspired our advocacy as described in Chapter 8.

Resettling children with their relatives is often cited as the best way to fulfil a vision for a reduction in the numbers of street children or for a city with no street dwellers. It meets some donors' demands for a non-institutional or family-based response which not only provides the preferred environment for a child to develop but can tick the boxes for sustainability and participation. Although this section may have a cynical tone so far, it is also a realistic view of the context in which we may find ourselves 'doing resettlement'. Being aware of external pressures and perhaps conflicting motives and assumptions prepares us to check our own motives, establish our aims, plan effective service delivery and explain or defend it. Other agendas may tempt us to cut corners or speed up the resettlement process to such an extent that we are wasting our time – street children **will** return to the street if this part of our work is not done carefully and thoroughly. It takes time and costs both in terms of human and financial resources. *If* you are still interested – read on.

Thomas Feeny explores the concept and practise of family reunification and makes the point that there are gaps that need to be filled:

> Unfortunately, the most important question of methodology – **how** this reunification process should best be performed – remains unclear.
>
> Feeny, 2005

This section is about methodology – how to resettle, reconcile or reunite street children with their relatives. It is *a* methodology rather than *the* methodology (which I don't believe exists) and is based on what we learned in Uganda over a specific period of time. However, the vision, insight and thought behind it came from hearing about and witnessing what others had done, transferring lessons from elsewhere and reacting to what we discovered. Resettlement journeys that ranged from a few hours to several days provided time and opportunity to discuss the process, dynamics, anomalies and outcomes of each situation.

The long hours, unpredictable events, sometimes dangerous situations and the emotional intensity of resettlement work were insignificant compared to the experience and often the joy of being with a street child before and during the process of reconciliation. Some resettlements involved extraordinary scenes; disbelief turned to joy when a mother, who thought her son was dead, realised he was home, faces lit up as siblings were reunited and a young man, fully aware of harsh realities on the street, realised that forgiveness offered by a previously hostile parent made true reconciliation possible. Other attempts to reconcile street children and relatives were equally dramatic for other reasons: being chased from a village by an angry mob who believed that the child was to blame for a relatives death, realising children who had been involved in rituals associated with witchcraft were not welcome, sharing the sharp pain a child felt when he discovered that the one relative he knew would welcome him back, had died months before. Not all of the resettlements I carried out with Ugandan social work staff were as remarkable as the ones mentioned but most were significant and special and I felt privileged to be involved.

Although each social context and organisation is unique, the following pages should stimulate thought and introduce principles and points of reference to consider when planning or strengthening resettlement programmes. Accounts of resettlement work in various countries confirm that no two stories are the same but there are common areas and principles to consider, skills and lessons to be learned from each other.

I learned about a 13-year-old street girl in Bolivia, made pregnant by an older street boy and now resettled with an older sister. Both girls were supported in many ways and enabled to run a small fruit juice business to fund further schooling and childcare.

An organisation in India shared an experience of a very young child who was trafficked to Hyderabad and then abandoned. He hardly spoke for 15 days and then offered very little detail in regard to his family and origin. Staff built trust and a good rapport with the child and were able to gain snippets of information about food, language and prayers he remembered, to narrow down the search. With help from police records and staff willing to travel to Mumbai, the family was traced. At the time of reuniting the child with his family staff were able to sensitise and educate about the risks of trafficking.

A recent resettlement in Ethiopia revealed the complexity of family breakdown. Hassan's father remarried just two months after the death of Hassan's mother. He was probably still grieving when he was expected to address another woman as 'mother'. Their relationship was tense from the beginning. The process of reconciliation was handled sensitively and it took 18 months. Visits and contact built slowly and allowed for relationships to be renewed or develop – with his father, with neighbours and former playmates and with his stepmother. The organisation continues to visit and support in various ways. Within every setting, each story and set of relationships is unique. Every resettlement experience is worth reflecting upon to discover:

- What went well?
- What surprised you about this experience?
- What could have been done differently?
- What was specific to this situation, context, culture or family?
- What are the main features of this example and what can we learn from it?

The purpose of resettling or attempting to resettle street children should correspond to and reflect the core values, beliefs or principles, the vision and mission statement of the organisation.

Our core beliefs in the uniqueness and intrinsic value of every child, in the role of family and community, in the provision of safe environment to enable growth and development and the overall mandate to protect every child informed and inspired our aim to resettle street children with their relatives. Of course reconciliation or reunification was not feasible or desirable in cases where children had run from abusive situations or where growth and development would be hindered as a result of returning to relatives.

Process and impact

The process of resettlement has inherent value and this should be expressed in our understanding of 'success' and impact. The process may enable a child to understand his journey, to reconnect even in small ways with people from his background and to develop awareness of his past *even if* they do not reintegrate or resettle as planned or hoped for. The child who has benefitted in these and other ways may be able to connect in a more meaningful way later on in life or when specific circumstances alter. In that sense, the process has been successful and should not be disregarded as a 'failed resettlement'. Donors may ask for success rates according to a very narrow definition of success so practitioners should be ready to explain and educate about the value of the process itself and reflect this in reporting along with lessons learned. Before the process begins an organisation should ask:

- Do we have personnel equipped and available for this kind of work?
- What are the implications in terms of time?
- Do we have the financial resource to meet the demands and expectations of the process fully and to avoid disappointment?

In Chapter 6 core social work competencies are considered many of which are essential for the resettlement process. Availability is also a key issue. Resettlement will not work as an 'add-on' or extra but demands designated and trained staff. Team members need to be responsive and flexible and able to critically reflect on each part of the process and the journey as a whole.

I was asked recently how much time an 'average' resettlement takes. It was an excellent question and reflected the amount of thought that was going into planning. First contact with a street child or at least first indication that resettlement is a possibility to first visit with the family could be as little as a week if a child, recently lost or abandoned in the city, is desperate to get home and especially vulnerable. For example:

> A former street child on our junior management team introduced us to a 'new arrival' called Roger. Roger's mother had married several times often to violent men. She arranged for him to be looked after by an uncle without realising the pressures and conditions he was living in so Roger was forced to live on the street. Within a week of meeting Roger, we located his mother who had moved to another city. The situation was complex and his mother needed reassurance and support to protect both herself and Roger but reconciliation and resettlement happened within a matter of weeks.

More commonly, it took several months of careful planning and preparation before an initial visit was made. My answer was given reluctantly as there are endless variables and each approach differs. Concurring with an expert in South America, I responded that it *may* take months and possibly years. Speeding up the process invariably led to information being missed, situations not being dealt with properly and either a higher chance of a child returning to the street or worse still being placed or returned to difficult or abusive situations. None of those are desirable outcomes. A much better return on investment – to use commercial parlance – is achieved by only doing the number of resettlements you can do *well*.

The same principle applies to financial resource implications. Costs may be reduced by using public transport or by doing multiple resettlements in one journey. However, there are risks and limitations which may jeopardise the outcome and prove more costly in the end. Some organisations take large groups to one region at a time. As well as questioning how thorough the assessment and preparation has been, I wonder about the impact of perceiving that you are simply one of many being transported to a particular region at a convenient time. Reuniting children and relatives, dealing with past events, offering encouragement, practical or financial assistance all take time and demand attention if the reintegration is going to last. Experience showed that this could only be given if a maximum of two – possibly three – children were taken on each resettlement journey.

We have considered the context and pressures to 'do resettlement', our motivations and the purposes of reconciling street children with their families and the need to redefine and broaden our understanding of 'success' in relation to resettlement as a process. Financial, time and human resource implications are significant but so are the risks of cutting corners, doing resettlement in a half-hearted way, compromising or rushing in order to meet donor demands. The following resettlement process outlined assumes commitment, time, finance and either the skills to do it well or the framework and resources to develop such abilities.

Initiating the process

Positioning resettlement within a wider programme

How and when the process of resettlement is initiated depends on its position within an organisation's overall approach and programme. For example, we collaborated with an agency whose sole activity with street children was resettlement. Street children knew that resettlement was the agency's intention for them from the outset. The agency made contact with street children in remand homes or had children referred to them specifically for resettlement.

In our organisation, resettlement was 'positioned' differently. Although we were regularly in and out of remand homes, prison and police stations, it was not to identify children needing or asking to be resettled with relatives. As outlined in Chapter 3 on relational work, having entered their 'world' and formed an authentic relationship, we engaged with street children on their territory. In that context the possibility of resettlement was explored. Other options were available and street children were aware that resettlement was *an* activity not the sole activity of the project.

I worked with another project at the beginning of its work when resettlement was on offer before other services had been fully developed. It was interesting to note that almost every child contacted *said* they wanted to be resettled. There was a rush of resettlement visits and journeys made but six months later many children had returned to the city. Why? Did they genuinely want to go home or did they simply want attention and any assistance going?

In our experience word spread quickly about who offered what and about the expectations and requirements for getting attention or assistance. Enterprising street children adjusted their stories and responses according to what a project offered. When resettlement is one of many possible outcomes it influences responses and choices made particularly within a holistic and relational context. The aim should be to get a truthful, accurate and comprehensive picture of the child, their background, needs and circumstances. The way we 'position' and initiate the process of resettlement can assist us in fulfilling this aim.

Initial thoughts of going home

Thinking about resettlement may begin generally and informally when a street child witnesses one of his friends being taken home.

> Kisakye is a boy who only considered the possibility of attempting to reconcile with his family when his friend Hamsa made that decision for himself. Hamsa had been on the street longer than Kisakye and seemed better able to cope with the demands and risks of street life so it surprised many of us when he expressed a desire to go home. At a much later stage, Kisakye participated in a follow up visit to the home of Hamsa which reinforced the decision he had made by then to return to his village and people.

There was a celebratory air as children left either the drop in centre or halfway home to be resettled. Many children being resettled asked team members to pray for them or their family – reflecting not just the potential hazards of any long distance travel in Uganda but the challenges and uncertainties that lay ahead. These occasions prompted on-lookers or friends to review their own situation and wishes.

Motivation

At this stage the worker must establish what the *motivation* for wanting to go home is. It may seem obvious when predictable answers are given such as 'I am tired of the street' or 'I need to see my mother' but it is important to invest time and skill discovering what lies beyond and behind responses.

The forum for introducing the idea of resettlement is significant. We avoided using general meetings with large groups of lads to talk about resettlement. If a group of lads were asked how many of them would like to return to their village almost all of them would put up their hands. They did so to give the enquirer what they wanted to hear or to save face in front of peers or because it offered the chance of a break from the city. When we were lackadaisical in initiating and planning resettlements, I am convinced we took children and young people who simply wanted outings to other parts of the country. They never intended to stay and sometimes got back to the city before we did!

The best forum for introducing the idea and explaining the process of resettlement was counselling or individual work with children. Even when a child requested to see us about being resettled, initial conversations steered and enabled a child to tell their whole story rather than assuming resettlement would be the eventual outcome. Some may be curious about relatives not seen for a long time but a visit may not be appropriate. This is more likely to become clear in the context of ongoing relational work with a key worker than in chance conversations or a group setting. We designed a simple form to remind us to cover certain areas in initial discussions. There is a danger in all social work of forms hindering the information gathering process. They can be used to avoid going deeper and further. A weary relational worker may be tempted to hide behind a list of questions and be content with one or two word answers rather than using them as tools for triggering and encouraging narrative which reveals quality information. It may take several significant conversations to establish resettlement may be a possibility and care and patience at this stage will save time, energy and finance in the long run.

Typically there were several reasons for wanting to go home. Weariness of street life and curiosity about home may both have increased over time. The latter may, as described above, have been prompted by another child's experience. There may have been one or several disappointments or dashed hopes. Fresh information from the village may have been received. We were often amazed at how messages got relayed thanks to the vast network of minibuses across the country. It has been surpassed only by the rapid increase in mobile phone services across Africa. Changes in perspective as children grow and develop also contribute to understanding why they may want to go home. There should be both negative and positive reasons. Going home may be seen as a means of escaping general or specific difficulties but it is important to find constructive motivation too. Reintegration and village life itself may be more difficult than anticipated so there needs to be aspiration and determination.

Participation

We have considered how resettlement relates to the wider approach and activity of a project or organisation, the initial thoughts of going home and the motivation behind an expressed desire to resettle. All of these are significant in initiating the process of reconciling children with their families and the participation of the child is critical throughout. In other words, resettlement should not be seen as a prearranged outcome or formulaic response to a child being and living on the street. The initiation needs to come from the child as much as the worker. The worker's role is to facilitate and empower the child to lead and understand the process and to grasp the consequences of choices made. That will lead to greater sense of ownership and responsibility for outcomes and the level of cooperation needed to ensure time and money is well spent.

Assessment or forming a hypothesis

The purpose and process of making an assessment or forming a hypothesis was described as a core element of a *relational* approach. This should be applied to the resettlement process once it is considered a possible outcome.

Gathering information and understanding culture

Information should be gathered in the ways described earlier through observation, active listening and the worker using skills in empathy to see the world and understand the past as the child does. Even in the northern hemisphere where extended families are less common, the complexity of family life can lead to confusion. We found that questions needed to be asked in several ways and feedback given to clarify who related to who and how. Working cross-culturally demands an awareness of terminology and significance attached to relationships which may differ from what we are used to. Cousins were referred to as 'brothers' or 'sisters', an uncle may be 'my young father' and in families where there had been multiple marriages, breakdown or death it took time and patience to get the facts. What appeared to be a self-contradicting account at first made far more sense later on when we realised there had been three fathers and that one of them was actually an uncle. Even then there were often surprises when we arrived at a child's home. It was important to be well advised on anomalies and seemingly incongruent details early on.

Assimilating information and analysing risk

Methods have been described for assimilating information and considering the ideas and wishes of children as they are empowered to tell their stories. Exploring resettlement should involve some life story work using tools such as 'The Road of Life' to help both child and worker understand the journey so far. Signs, symbols and faces can be used to attach emotional responses to people or events. These enable the worker to analyse the story and the risks of attempting to reconcile a child with relatives. They may provide indicators of whether a resettlement is even worth attempting. Stories or manifestations of abuse may arise and need to be handled sensitively – if possible by more than one worker. It may be that the risk of returning a child to a harmful situation is simply too great. The process may have been important in the therapeutic process for dealing with trauma and hurt or it may be that the young person is no longer traumatised by previous events so revisiting them is unwise. In Uganda, if the child and family were separated several years before, an abusive relative may have died or left home which meant reuniting the child with surviving relatives was worth pursuing.

Testing hypotheses and working with others

Assessment involves gathering and interpreting information and making decisions based on that information. Social workers with street children should not shy away from a forensic approach, considering possibilities and testing them out to reach a hypothesis. Verifying information is crucial with the child and with peers and workers from other areas. Does the story, even with all permutations and possibilities, 'add up'? Are accounts plausible and consistent? Places and events need to be established as fully as possible. In our staff team we had members from all over Uganda so we were able to cross check regional, cultural or geographical information. We made frequent visits to remote areas as well as major towns so we could enquire about families and events. We collaborated with NGOs in other areas and were able to ask for details to be confirmed or clarified. Of course there were times when we had little or no knowledge other than what the child had told us and in areas where transport and communications are limited that will often be the case.

Preparing the ground

Street children often experience disappointment. It is crucial not to add to that experience so the period after initiating the idea of resettlement and making an assessment should be regarded as preparation. If there is enough indication that resettlement is possible the following questions should be asked:

What needs to be done immediately and by whom?

Seguya had lived on the street for nine years when he asked us to seriously consider taking him home. There were several issues that needed to be dealt with immediately. He had a sexually transmitted illness which needed dealing with along with associated behaviour and relationships. Previous attempts at vocational training had not gone well so there was an immediate need to address the issues that had led to his suspension from college. Some further research was needed about his home area and family background and some of the facts about current circumstances needed verifying. Seguya was compliant with these tasks.

What conditions need to be met or benchmarks set?

Ssekimpi had been in a series of fights that may have been a result of bullying. He was affected by a speech impediment and low self-esteem. A period of stability was needed and he was allowed to stay at the 'refuge' which existed in part for boys preparing to go home. During that time he committed to assisting in various areas and attending at least some lessons at the Learning Centre.

The behaviour and lifestyle of street children sometimes reflect the struggle to survive on the street but needs to change before attempting to resettle them. Amongst relatives we encountered great fear that children who had run away and experienced street life would 'infect' a village or other children in it with 'bad habits'. If we knew that lads had been aggressive, heavily influenced by drugs or alcohol or erratic and unreliable, steps were taken to enable and encourage them to change prior to even attempting reconciliation.

What should the time frame be and is there agreement to stick to it?

The illustrations and concerns above imply that there is no fixed answer to this question but workers were encouraged to propose a time frame depending on the conditions and changes expected. Although fixing a date for an initial visit may not be possible or appropriate at this stage, specifying a period of time to prepare reassures street children that they are being taken seriously. Unless there were serious concerns or gaps in information or understanding this would normally be three to four months or the equivalent of a school term.

Forming a plan

Using information gathered and hypotheses formed, the next stage involved brainstorming all possibilities with the street child. With the child, we imagined changes at home, the impact of having been away, we discussed siblings and how old they would now be and the possible responses to both the child and his family seeing each other again. We discovered even in rural areas, where time seemed to stand still, that people and circumstances changed. For example, parents had remarried, a father had suffered from a stroke, relatives had died or relocated. All these affected the process so possibilities had to be aired.

At times these discussions led to a change of plan – from going to one area of the country or a specific relative to another. Once boys knew that going home was a possibility some would send messages asking for information from the village. If new information arose, wishes and plans sometimes altered.

Lads needed to be clear on what the consequences of certain decisions might be. Sometimes, changes in behaviour and lifestyle had to be made and adhered to if they were to survive village and family life. Of course the family would also be expected to change and deal with issues. The child needs to be assured that he is not to 'blame' for circumstances leading to separation and that all parties would share responsibility for the planned outcome. Once these were understood, a 'resettlement plan' was made and included the following elements:

- An initial visit to a relative or village on an agreed date.
- A commitment to find out more about the family and their perspective.
- An agreement to share experience of living on the street.
- Exploring and, if relevant, working to resolve specific issues. In some cases, street children believed they had done something to anger relatives or knew they were suspected of theft or causing damage to property. These specific incidents needed to be addressed. Sometimes there had been a misunderstanding or the event was far less important in the minds of the relatives than the child had supposed it would be.
- Defining what support was necessary at the outset. Almost without exception children identified immediate needs to enable them to stay at home. Some organisations provide a standard resettlement kit which may include bedding, utensils, food, tools and so on. Our concerns about kits stemmed from reports of children cooperating with resettlement plans knowing they would receive a kit which could then be sold and more frequently reports of families who either sold them or gave them to members of the family they felt were more

'deserving' than the former street child. Our approach was to ensure that purchasing necessary items was done in a non-formulaic way.

- Investigating options for schooling, training, business or agriculture.
- Support needs at least for the first academic term or year.
- Identifying who is responsible for which aspects of the resettlement visit.
- Listing information needed and whether other staff members were to be involved.
- An understanding of what was expected and how progress was to be monitored through contact, follow up and reporting.

In our setting, approval for a resettlement plan was given by senior leaders who would agree the process and budget and hold staff to account for time and finances incurred. This may sound obvious but children and their families need certainty that all aspects of the process have been agreed and delivered. Accountability should provide such certainty.

Testing the hypothesis again

Prior to the initial visit we allocated time to test any hypothesis formed. We asked ourselves:

- Has new information been revealed during the preparation period?
- What has the response been to the resettlement plan?
- Has the child or young person's behaviour changed?
- Are there signs of anxiety or excitement about returning home?
- Has the child or young person met expectations and demonstrated their commitment to the process and plan?
- Have other key players and peers responded positively or offered new information which may be useful?

Answers and responses to the above enabled us to go ahead, to delay or withdraw the proposal to visit the home of a street child.

Initial visit

Some organisations in contexts where transport and communications are effective may have already made 'pre-visits' to a child's relatives. We were challenged by an international donor's insistence that *no* child should be resettled unless staff from an organisation had been to the home beforehand. I visited organisations in South Africa which always made contact with the families prior to resettlement through local social welfare offices or other agencies and almost always conducted pre-visits. In the Ugandan context, and I suspect others, that was simply not viable. There were dozens of occasions when, even with the child in the vehicle, we spent long hours trying to locate the exact village or hut that their family lived in. Sometimes directions included crossing banana plantations that had long been dug up and replaced with other crops or referenced trees that were not quite where the child remembered. Times have changed and assuming a child has contact details, it is easier to telephone a family ahead of a proposed visit than it was ten years ago but it may not necessarily be the wisest course of action.

Having the child with us on first contact sometimes meant that we were able to trace the home and probably led to a better reception and outcome. Relatives may make assumptions about children who have lived on the street. This is referred to above, concerning behaviour and lifestyle and some assumptions are justifiable, but seeing and hearing their child enables relatives to see them as they really are and not how they imagine they might have become. Imagine the day has arrived. Preparations included in the plan have been made and expectations met.

Introductions and expectations

If the child was anxious or requested us to do so, we would first approach the family without him. During a long journey a lad's mood may have changed from excitement at leaving Kampala to thoughtful anticipation of what lay ahead to fear about the response of parents or other relatives to seeing him. If he requested to do so, the lad remained in the vehicle while one or both workers approached the home and introduced themselves.

Greetings

Greet as the culture dictates. In Africa greetings are of huge importance and put people at ease. The main Baganda greeting is a sequence of questions, responses, pauses and affirmative gestures which are then repeated. If anyone new appears during the sequence, it starts again and the newcomer is included. It takes time and often when I thought we were getting to the end and could move on to our purpose and intent someone would join us and we would begin all over again. It would have been futile to short-circuit the process, as it is part of being welcomed to the home. The visitor finally asks 'Eradde?' which literally means 'Is everything calm here?' and the word is repeated to indicate it is. All of that happens outside the home itself – on the baraza or plot of land in front of it. Once inside another series of questions and greetings occur, establishing who the main host is and that they welcome the visitors. The urgency and significance of the journey did not outweigh the importance of this settling in process. If the child was with us and there was some shock or surprise, introductory remarks about our intent may have been offered prior to the traditional greetings but without exception they were allowed to run their course. In a few instances the reaction to first seeing the child was negative and extreme and we will consider that later. At times there was jubilant joy and tears as child and parent were reunited and traditional greetings were suspended.

> Sadiq was assumed dead by his mother when we eventually found her in the market where she worked. It was not the first time a relative had thought they were seeing a ghost so there were conflicting emotions of fear and excitement. Friends reassured the gracious older Muslim lady that all was well and her long lost son was truly standing before her. Once calm, she was able to greet and welcome us before settling down to conversation. For Sadiq it was the start of a journey that would take him back to other relatives in Rwanda.

Community

I mentioned passers-by, neighbours and friends above. The wider community is significant in parts of Africa and may provide additional support for the resettlement process to be effective. A neighbour or local leader often helped us get a clearer picture of general and specific issues and circumstances affecting the family. Their involvement was usually welcomed, unlike some families in difficult circumstances I worked with in UK who felt their privacy was to be protected uncompromisingly.

Sharing

At this stage we tried to provide an opportunity for both family and the child being resettled to share something of their journey and experience. Before giving away too much information, it was important to find out what the family understood or believed had happened. If it felt appropriate, we would ask 'Where do you think your child has been and what do you suppose he has been doing?'

It was interesting to hear their response and to watch the child's reaction. Some families had no idea where a child had been or had a very different understanding of what he had been doing. They may have heard snippets of information leading them to conclude all was well or that their son was living rough or had got in to trouble with the law. They may have simply imagined a very different scenario to what actually happened. The intention should be to provide as accurate a picture as possible of the journey their child has experienced since they last met.

One peer organisation used shock tactics at this stage of the process. They had an album of photos showing some of the worst aspects of street life – scavenging from bins, fighting, pictures of infected wounds and so on. They would wait to hear what the relatives thought the child had experienced and then show them the album to educate them about street life and what their child had or might have seen. They found this technique to be effective. We preferred to communicate some of the realities of street life in other ways over the course of a natural conversation. The point they were making was valid though – the streets of the city were not paved with gold, there weren't immediate opportunities for work or, as one family believed, people handing out cash to new arrivals in the city! Myths about urban life still exist and workers with street children should utilise opportunities to inform and advocate for a more realistic view.

Stigma

There may be stigma associated with street children, and workers were encouraged to be aware of and attempt to deal with it. Having shared background and understanding of what both child and family had experienced, some families were alarmed or fearful at the thought of their child having been on the street. Some believed that the child would bring shame on them or that habits learnt on the street were for life and would contaminate the village. At times this was expressed verbally but more commonly it was revealed indirectly or at a later stage. We proactively addressed this by:

- Ensuring boys were well dressed, clean and polite on first meeting. This was a realistic way of reducing the risk of stigma hindering the process from the outset.
- Boys were encouraged to share some positive experiences they had and details of any schooling, training or other activities they had been involved with. We knew that initial information given would be picked up in conversation, often around the fire, once we had left. One social worker used to laugh just thinking about how long the family and child would be awake talking about experiences and changes in their lives.
- Informing the family about the programme at the drop in centre, refuge or halfway home to assure them that the child had not literally come from the street. They had been preparing to come home and meeting expectations in the process.

Roles and responsibilities

The last point mentioned led naturally to discussing roles and responsibilities. It was important to emphasise that the way we could now help was to support the child to remain at home. Families needed to grasp not only that the street environment hindered a child's growth and development but that relatives had primary responsibility for his care and protection. There was as much need for parents or relatives to cooperate, to adjust or change certain behaviour and arrangements as for the child to demonstrate commitment to making reconciliation work.

Some families did not seem at all interested in what other services the organisation offered and we felt this was a positive indicator about the resettlement's sustainability. Sadly that was not always the case and conversations later on revealed that they wanted others to look after the child or expected him to return to benefit from the organisation. To prevent this expectation we would allude to reintegration with the family as the only option available.

The desired outcome at this stage was relatives' understanding and desiring to fulfil their role to parent the child. The difficulties faced that had led to breakdown or misunderstanding had to be acknowledged but we also communicated that the outcome was so important to us that we would offer whatever support we could to make it happen.

A four-way plan

Following introductions, sharing and learning from each other and establishing expectations around roles and responsibilities, it was important to agree about the purpose of the visit and the way ahead. We kept paper work to a minimum because firstly, it was associated with a formality that may have increased suspicion or prevented genuine sharing and secondly, with low levels of literacy we did not want to cause embarrassment or assume by leaving written documents that we had effectively communicated what needed to be said. Sometimes staff members from the local school or council were present and were more open to reading and signing an agreement or plan on behalf of the family. That said, it was essential for accountability and follow up that anything agreed was recorded by the organisation staff at the time of or immediately after the visit.

The plan at this stage was four way between the child, the organisation, the family and the wider community. The family, in the context of the community and with support from the organisation, was expected to safeguard the child and enable him to reach his potential. Core elements of a plan included:

- *Common aims* for child and family so that there was clarity about what we hoped to achieve.
- *Communications* between family members, with community leaders and between the family and the project. One difference over the years since we started working with street children is the use of mobile telephones to enable contact to continue especially in the first few months of a child being resettled. Some agencies formalise this with an initial agreement to communicate at specific times.
- *Level and nature of support* which, as mentioned in relation to resettlement 'kits', was not formulaic but responsive to the specific family's circumstances, attitude and response. It was important to be specific and diligent in channelling support as agreed. In most cases we offered support – either financial or practical – to ensure a child could attend school and that the family was no worse off as a result of the reconciliation that had occurred. Initial visits often included visits to a school and brainstorming possible ventures that may raise a family's income. The first term's fees – which in our setting decreased after the introduction of universal primary education – were sometimes paid directly to the local school. Fees excluded the costs of lunch, uniforms, books and equipment which had to be found elsewhere. Ensuring these were purchased with money entrusted was one measure of commitment to the process.
- *Defining and measuring commitment* to the resettlement process. This included tangible responses like buying uniform or preparing an enclosure for livestock to be bought at a later stage. It also included child development indicators and the quality of relationships within the home. Questions were asked if the child resettled was being treated differently from siblings – maybe in the hours and nature of domestic work or where he is expected to sleep. There were either reasonable practical explanations or answers which indicated that he was being marginalised.
- *Setting a time frame* proved to be important to assure families of continued support and enable them to meet specific and realistic expectations. Knowing that we would return within a specific period gave the impetus to work hard and reduced the likelihood of the child simply running back to the city when problems arose.
- *Keeping safeguarding paramount* so that indicators of abuse of any form were looked for and responded to. There were times when observation or information gathering gave cause for alarm and a child returned with us to the city. This was rare due to the preparation period referred to earlier, which aimed to 'filter out' children who would return to an abusive situation.

Follow up and exit strategy

A core element
'Follow up' – ongoing visits to the home after a child has been reconciled with his family – is at the very heart of effective resettlement and yet is often the weakest aspect of it. Once a

child is no longer physically before us and other pressures arise, it is tempting to neglect this part of the process. To do so is to fail the child and those who have enabled us to do this work. It is the key to resettlement being sustained and is the only way an organisation can measure its impact in this area. I worked alongside leaders of an organisation claiming a 90 per cent success rate for over two thousand resettlements carried out. I discovered that unless a child re-appeared at their offices in the capital they regarded the case as a 'successful resettlement'. I was dismayed at this – the offices were outside the city centre and rarely frequented by street children and figures failed to account for those who may have run away from home but felt too ashamed to inform or show face at the project. With little regular presence on the street by day let alone night, I felt it likely that their statistics were over generous. The only way to be *absolutely* sure a child has remained with his relatives, ideally settled and thriving, is to return in person.

Clear commitment and expectations

This sounds like repetition because it is. Whatever the level and nature of support is at this stage it should be accompanied by two-way commitment and agreed expectations. Every follow up visit will differ according to anticipated and unexpected circumstances, the transition process and other factors. The first follow up visit was ordinarily 12 weeks after the initial visit. When possible it would coincide with the beginning or ending of academic terms so that progress could be monitored both at school and home and preparations made for the following term.

Income generating activities

If the family had been left with a task – the example of making an enclosure for animals is a good one – progress on that could be measured and the next phase agreed on. The most common income generating activity was rearing livestock and when feasible we utilised what was already in place and strengthened or added to it. With one extra healthy person in the mix productivity increased and family income rose. Other examples included chapatti making, selling clothes or local produce, drying and selling fish and in one case developing a small pharmacy business. One family agreed that the mother would prepare the ingredients and cook chapattis during the day enabling the child to sell them in the evening. Each case needed to be assessed and the level of support agreed upon.

Further follow up

Further visits will differ from the first and are equally important. The frequency and regularity needs to be established according to the overall 'exit strategy'. Unexpected events such as death or illness in the family put added strain on families and in some cases follow up continued for years rather than months. Our approach was flexible enough to allow this but others prefer to be prescriptive in the length of time and nature of follow up. Either way, the purpose should be to review the integration of the child and reflect on change and progress.

Problem-solving and phased withdrawal

These went hand in hand. As the family's capacity to solve problems increased so did the possibility of a phased withdrawal of support. The locus of control had to shift from the project to relatives as they assumed responsibility for and care of the child. Dealing with medical problems, issues at school or with behaviour needed to be tackled without recourse to the project or organisation. Clearly stated reasons were needed for the organisation to continue following up after two years. By then income generation and problem solving should have enabled a reunited family to function without external support.

Key issues in resettlement

An overview of our methodology of resettling street children has been given after considering its purpose and intrinsic value as a process. It is worth highlighting some considerations, issues and questions surrounding the work of resettlement some of which have been incorporated above.

Context

Never underestimate the importance of understanding the context within which street children are resettled. Those working cross-culturally have to develop empathy and be receptive to new ways of thinking and doing. The following are worth considering:

- *What is the legal framework you are operating within?* In our situation, laws reflected an aspiration to hold parents to account and to protect the best interests of the child. However it was a resource-constrained environment with little if any activity in terms of child safeguarding. We did discover that a local government official was mandated with the task of child welfare and protection and occasionally used this knowledge to encourage them to take an interest in families where children had been resettled. Readers may be considering or are already working in similar settings.
- *Are there Government expectations in relation to resettlement?* It was extremely useful at times to refer to the Best Practice Guidelines produced by the government in conjunction with UNICEF. In fact we had participated in writing these guidelines and much of the content reflected our thinking and vision but they gave credence to the methodology outlined above. They promoted the idea that there was no quick-fix solution to resettling street children and that it had to be done methodically and carefully or not at all.
- *What aspects of local, regional or tribal culture are pertinent in each case?* This was especially important for resettling outside of the central region where the capital was located. Geographical considerations such as terrain, climate, local resources and so forth were often important in planning and being aware of issues facing the area and residents. Areas facing drought on a regular basis had specific needs and seasonal struggles. It was useful to know what crops grew when and whether an area was renowned for certain produce or livestock. If a child is returning to an area where fishing is the main means of livelihood net-mending or fishing skills may equip him to contribute to the welfare of the family more than pig-rearing or horticulture.

Infrastructure has been mentioned in relation to communications and transport which are significant for planning visits but also to understand an area. Its accessibility and resources relate to employment and opportunity. Many of the above will relate to and determine the socio-economic situation of an area or the family being worked with. Further information may be available from community development agencies, which brings us on to the next key issue.

Collaboration

Collaboration takes time and effort but is a key element in effectively resettling street children. To reiterate what has already been covered – community leaders, the wider family and neighbours, social welfare, local council or probation services and other NGOs should all be considered as potential partners. We found that working openly with leaders and neighbours led to awareness and support being offered. It reassured the family and child that others in the area were aware of the challenges they faced and ensured some local accountability for progress made.

On resettlement journeys we encountered events and changes that were impossible to predict. It is worth being 'RFA' – ready for anything! Illness, death and other demands arose. There will be times when information given turns out to be inaccurate or incomplete. Sometimes information will have been left out intentionally. Our approach intended to be flexible and non-formulaic. The process was as important as the end product and was potentially as valuable.

Summary

If donors demand a quick-fix solution or a pre-determined one-size-fits-all response to children needing and hoping to be reconciled and resettled with their families, practitioners need to inform and educate that such things will result in money and time wasted. Thomas Feeny draws a similar conclusion in his paper on family reunification:

> It is very likely a misuse of funds and distortion of donor intent to pursue a fashionable idea that has little grounding in the reality of policy, methodology or the complex reality of street children's lives.

Feeny, 2005

Of course family reunification of street children is not necessarily the best way forward for all street children. Feeny rightly points this out and highlights cultural assumptions and stereotypes that must be tackled prior to any work with street children and in particular reuniting children with relatives. However, this section is borne out of experience which enabled us to develop and ensure reunification was more than a 'fashionable idea'. Many vital lessons were learned in regard to:

- Clarifying the purpose of resettlement generally and of each individual journey made.
- Viewing the process as important or more so than the end 'product'.
- Ensuring child participation is not tokenistic by working in accordance with the child's desire and understanding.

- Assessing, planning and preparing thoroughly.
- Initial visits to families and the significance of agreed plans.
- Regarding 'follow up' as the heart of the process rather than an added extra.
- The key issues of context, collaboration and dealing with the unexpected.

A methodology evolved which embraced the complexity of street children's lives, upheld their rights, respected their decisions and proved that, if done carefully and thoroughly, the work and experience of reconciling and resettling street children with their families is extremely worthwhile, poignant and rewarding.

Appendix 5. Integration into existing families (The Foster Care Scheme)

Introduction

The fifth aspect of an approach aiming to be 'transitional' is foster care. There is confusion in countries where it is a relatively new phenomenon as to what it actually means. The phrase has been used – wrongly in my opinion – to refer to family-style institutional care. Some organisations recognise the limitations of large dormitory style accommodation and divide children into smaller units often under the care and supervision of a house 'parent'. This is *not* foster care. It has been encouraging to be approached by leaders of institutions who acknowledge that and want to know more. Definitions of foster care refer to the act of providing family life for children and may state why there is a need for it. Foster Care Associates describes it as, 'a way of providing family life for someone else's child in your own home when they are unable to live with their own birth family' and for our purposes we went for a similar definition in our introductory literature.

Foster care is provided when a child is welcomed into an existing home and is integrated into the life of that home. They are offered security, support and loving relationship in order to grow and develop.

In the last section it was clearly stated that not *every* child can or should be encouraged to return to their relatives. As the project in Uganda developed, there was an increasing need to address the difficulties faced by younger street children. With outreach focussed on football and a reputation for welcoming and working with older children and teenagers, the emphasis in the first few years was on finding training opportunities or setting up micro-enterprises. Lads were taught skills and offered support to become independent over a period of time. An encounter with much younger children who could not be resettled led – almost by accident – to the first foster placement.

Taban and Jeremiah have been mentioned in Chapter 2 (page 33). Their story took an extraordinary turn when the project nurse noticed they were putting on weight rapidly and seemed to be growing in confidence. Fearing we would stop assisting them, they had not told us about a chance meeting with a lady in Nakasero market who was giving them breakfast in addition to the food they received after training at the Tigers Club. We were delighted to hear about acts of kindness in the community and arranged to meet the lady. Aisha was a widow whose surviving children had left home long ago. Others had died from HIV-related illness. During the previous weeks the boys had moved from the steps of a large office block to one of the more established depots. That meant we could easily find and monitor their progress but we were struggling to find a longer-term option. Many orphanages – even those who claimed to be working with street children – would not consider allowing two boys in directly from the street. We considered housing them ourselves but were advised against it by trusted Ugandan advisers. Apart from the need to go through arduous official processes, we were told it may distract from our core purpose and limit the numbers of children potentially helped during the years ahead. With hindsight that was wise advice. We continued to pray and search for a real alternative to the street. A period of building relationship with Aisha, significant conversations, visits to her home and meeting with friends and relatives of hers provided more background and reassurance that with support she could offer a loving home to both boys.

That was how we began facilitating informal foster care for street children. We were told it would not work.

Early development

When we set about designing and establishing the foster care scheme, we benefitted from the guidance and support of Fostering Network UK which was founded in 1974 as the National Foster Care Association. This was not because we were chasing a 'west-is-best' ideal in any way but because we wanted to learn from successes and failures and benefit from decades of experience. Foster care has existed in the UK for over seventy years and emerged following the work and findings of Victorian philanthropists. On 31st March 2010 there were 64,400 children being looked after by local government in England. 73% of these children (about 49,000) were in foster care and 2,300 were being placed for adoption (DfE, 2010). Relatively few were in residential care – secure homes, specialist schools or further education.

Stories of children in foster care with tragic outcomes hit the press in the UK fairly regularly. What the press largely ignores is the fact that tens of thousands of children who would otherwise be in situations of abuse and danger are in placements with incredibly hard-working families dedicated to the vision of children restored and potential released. During a meeting with the Fostering Network Director of Training, Cherie Talbot, I shared some of our experiences with just a handful of children and families. In response to her questions, I explained that if a child was being fostered by a family who were struggling to send their natural children to school we would consider their case and try to empower the family as a whole. If there was an immediate need that could be addressed we would. I gave the example of Moses whose new siblings were unable to go to school because the parents couldn't afford shoes for all their children. The project decided as a stopgap to provide shoes for all siblings to enable them to start school together with the child being fostered. The longer-term aim was for the family to be self-sufficient.

Cherie described some complexities of terms and conditions for foster carers in the UK and said it was refreshing to hear about our stage of development. The simplicity and implications of the story reminded her of the 'essence of foster care' and she wished it could be shared nationally. I returned to Uganda inspired to persist. During the first four years of operations there were just a few younger children placed with families who were mandated by the project to care for them. Recruitment of carers was through word of mouth by neighbours of existing foster carers, staff members and their contacts. When five children were looked after in this way we recruited Dinah, an experienced social worker, to increase our capacity.

With Cherie's assistance we were able to send Dinah to the UK for a month of training and experience with fostering teams and agencies in different parts of the country. What was universally relevant was brought back to strengthen and shape our planning and she wrote shortly after returning:

> It was so good to be able to learn from those who specialised in foster care for a very long time. I was struck by the way children were accepted in order to increase their self esteem and by the patience of social workers through problems and anger shown by children who had suffered abuse ... Areas of particular relevance to us in Kampala included the importance and involvement of men in foster care, skills in assessment, support and training of carers, record keeping and life stories, reducing stigmatisation of fostered children, connecting with natural families, sibling rivalry, taking children through their past, anger management and preparation of older children for independent living ... It has increased my excitement about all we do and are about to do.
>
> Dinah Mwesigye. *The Roar*, Spring 2005

Relation to the law

The foster care scheme remained 'informal' which reflected the lack of infrastructure and resources in relation to formal foster care services in Uganda. Much legislation relating to child welfare and protection was based on past English law and included provision of services and structures. The government lacked resources in terms of expertise, personnel and finance, and struggled to deliver the services that such legislation aspired to. Collaboration was challenging and there were only a few times when we were able to work in partnership with government agencies or through the courts to formalise foster care services. The legacy of some of Uganda's history was fear or at least suspicion of authority so we were advised to delay or limit mentioning courts or the probation service (which had responsibility for fostering and adoption services).

Our initial literature and documents stated clearly that the Tigers Club continued to assume responsibility for children fostered even though daily care had been assigned to carers who – unlike residential workers at the halfway home – were referred to as Tigers 'maamas' or 'taatas'. They were assessed and selected by the project for a specific placement following careful matching. Training, support and supervision would be provided by social workers appointed for these roles. In 2002 we wrote:

The project hopes that such arrangements will be recognised by the Courts and foster care arrangements formalised. Already some children have been formally fostered through the Wakiso District Court. The option of adoption can be seriously considered by the Courts after 36 months of placement. Foster carers are encouraged to view the arrangement as long term and to accept the possibility of a child remaining with the family until he or she is able to live independently.

Williams, 2002

Over the next five years we worked with around 40 children within the foster care scheme. Not all were placed and we encountered challenges we had not foreseen. Others have remained with foster families for a decade and are approaching adulthood with security and confidence.

The learning process was fascinating and we were particularly fortunate to be supported by a donor committed to learning as much as results or statistics produced. Foster care was – and still is – a new concept and the McKnight Foundation recognised that we were doing pioneer work. Every six months we wrote extensively of what had been learned and met with other beneficiaries to share experiences.

We later developed links with Substitute Families For Abandoned Children (SFAC) which is committed to enabling the implementation of foster care services in countries where it does not yet exist. Recent moves to develop foster care in Ethiopia have been inspired and guided by the experience in Uganda and services provided by SFAC.

Resources

The Fostering Network develops materials to assess, recruit, train and support foster carers. They are constantly improved and updated but at the time of initiating foster care in Uganda 'Skills to Foster' was the primary resource being used. I was struck by its relevance across cultures and was encouraged to use and adapt its content for use in Uganda. The founders of SFAC have extensive experience in foster care in the UK and recognise the value of making materials and resources available. Much of it has been adapted for use in other cultures and for lower to middle income countries. Of particular interest were countries where foster care had been dismissed as irrelevant or unworkable.

Subsequently we hosted the first regional training in foster care and welcomed 25 delegates from 12 organisations in five African countries to Kampala. Key concepts and components of foster care were taught by SFAC personnel and one of the most telling and encouraging comments received afterwards was:

I realise now we are not ready to launch a foster care programme. This work is too precious to do poorly. You have taught me what it means to be professional and I now know you either do this work properly or not at all.

Feedback from *Specialist Training in Foster Care*, Jan 2007

Other practitioners reviewed what they were doing, extended programmes, advocated for change in their organisations or took their first tentative steps in developing foster care as an option for street children.

The International Foster Care Organisation (IFCO) is a network dedicated to the promotion and support of family foster care all over the world. It exists to bring together those united by the aim to make the right of every child to live in a family a reality. Like SFAC, it offers networking, training and consultancy for those serious about initiating or developing foster care for street children.

Below is an outline of the programme which translated thinking and vision for foster care into practice. It reflected a desire to be professional and thorough and covered motivation, integration and acceptance, ongoing training, support and review.

Recruitment

The inevitable question people ask is 'Where do you find people willing to foster?' It is and never will be easy. There is a desperate shortage of foster carers in many parts of the world which is reflected in television and billboard advertising. In a context like Uganda, where foster care is comparatively new and already there are signs of misunderstanding about meanings and motivation, such vigorous marketing may not be appropriate. The story above illustrates how we virtually stumbled across the lady who would be the first foster carer or 'Tigers Maama'. The next three or four carers were personal links of staff or neighbours and even one staff member himself – who literally took his work home with him! He and his family continue to foster to this day. As the programme developed a recruitment strategy was needed which would incorporate and encourage the word-of-mouth approach we had previously depended upon. Using contacts already made as a starting point the foster care team:

- Extended invitations to open meetings about foster care.
- Visited key community and church leaders.
- Spoke at events and services about opportunities to foster.

A peer organisation decided to use the media by placing adverts and articles in newspapers and magazines and raising the profile of fostering and adoption on local television. Concerns about using that approach in our setting were that it may have opened the floodgates to people more interested in what might be gained than genuine commitment and it could have caused some to push their children away from home in order to get onto such a programme.

Over time the foster care social workers built a list of potential carers and shared information with the wider team about those coming forward. The following example of recruitment may have caused some raised eyebrows in another culture.

Patricia was a formidable, loving grandmother who had fostered Josiah for three years. We were introduced to her by a pastor known to a staff member and discovered that each of her five children had died – three from HIV related illness. Every grandchild except for one – a six year old called Moses – was cared for by other members of the family and she felt able and willing to welcome another child into her home. 'I have enough love for more' was how she put it to me. During the first year there were inevitable challenges for both Josiah and Patricia but with support and advice from social workers they persevered and soon began encouraging others to consider foster care. With great sadness Patricia passed away three years later. Many of us attended the funeral and were struck by the way neighbours and friends spoke of her selfless commitment to others less fortunate, even though she had so little. At her request a relative explained the foster care scheme instead of giving a eulogy. After the burial two neighbours (one in his eighties) and a relative came expressing genuine interest in becoming foster carers. I wondered at the time whether foster care recruitment at funerals of foster parents had been thought of before! Josiah was fostered by Patricia's cousin.

Assessment and selection

Once potential carers had been identified the process of assessing them began. If we knew of children waiting to be fostered, the temptation to rush this process was very real. On average it took three to four months of patiently building relationships and gathering information and insight to confirm a family's suitability to foster. That period of time is important to allow potential carers to understand fully what foster care involved and to consider all the implications and repercussions for each member of the household, for extended family and community. The influence and support of elders was vital for some foster placements to work and at times we should have been more diligent concerning this at assessment stage. New pressures, dynamics and in time joys will be experienced as both child and family adjust to a new situation. Dr Keith White urges caution in assuming foster care is *always* preferable to residential care and advocates for excellence in both. In an article called 'Ideology of Residential Care and Fostering' he reminds us that:

> Foster households . . . are not simply an extension of a 'normal' family; they are qualitatively different, and have their own potential and dynamics. They should be encouraged to flourish and grow.

> White, 2002

I believe that in all contexts what he says is true – foster families have their own potential and dynamics. Social workers need to enable and support families to discover and nurture that potential and those dynamics. To do that, social workers must be offered support, resources and space by project leaders and managers. When considering assessment and suitability to foster, workers should ensure families are aware that change *will* happen and look for indicators that they have the desire and capacity to embrace change. We adapted wording from the UK which articulated to potential carers what was and what wasn't important:

> There are many reasons why people are choosing to be Tigers Club foster carers.
>   Many families feel they would like to share the good things they have in their lives with a child who is unable to live at home or who does not have a family of their own. Applicants

do not have to be 'super-parents' although those with children of their own may feel they can offer another child what they have offered their own and thereby contribute positively to his or her life.

Foster carers need to like children and feel they have something to offer. They must value children and want to contribute towards their development and to protect them. Many carers appreciate that young people only have one childhood and that children need the contribution they are able to make.

There are strict criteria which applicants are expected to be meet. However, there are not many requirements that are fixed. Prospective carers do not need to be in a certain salary bracket, own a large home or have a certain standard of education. There is no 'ideal type'. Each family brings its own unique mixture of history, experiences, abilities and knowledge and uses them to help children and their families.

Williams, 2002

Workers were expected to be sure that a potential foster family's motives, understanding and values matched those described. They did this by examining relationships in the home, behaviour, priorities, responses given, feedback from relatives and neighbours' references. A series of discussions, interviews and eventually home visits were arranged to gather and verify information given and to help carers in their decision making process. The aim was to build a comprehensive profile of the family and the parenting environment. We did not impose a strict time frame but sought instead to allow space and time for further thought and wider discussion within families and between them and others in the community and neighbourhood. Potential carers were assured that at any time they could review and retract their decision without apology or embarrassment.

Of course basic criteria had to be met such as physical health and space for another child. Potential carers were told to expect the social worker to cover the following areas during the period of assessment:

Section 1
 Basic details
 You and your family
 Existing children
 Other children in the household
 Other adult members of the household
Section 2
 History and background
 Current partnerships and relationships
 Medical information
 Work and educational history
Section 3
 Family lifestyle

Rules of the home

Evidence of parenting behaviour and ability

Section 4

Accommodation, neighbourhood and mobility

Other key adult members of the community

Support networks such as faith-based communities, groups, friends

Section 5

Reasons and motives to foster

Any specific ages or circumstances to consider

Financial and other support expected or foreseen

Section 6

Compulsory checks to include medical questionnaire and if relevant documentation, criminal history, LC 1 Chairman recommendation

Personal referees to include where possible religious/community leaders, employers

Record of all meetings and home visits

Any particular placement concerns or information

Foster care social workers pooled ideas and shared information or concerns rather than working in isolation. A decision to select a particular carer or couple was usually made at a planning meeting ('baraza') as described earlier in the book. Sometimes social workers expressed concern even when criteria had been met and the areas above were all satisfactory. There would be an unease even though the cause of it was hard to identify. Intuition should be encouraged and attempts made to clarify the source of uncertainty perhaps by reviewing the process, bringing in another worker and allowing more time. After a period to reflect we reported:

> Despite many meetings and visits, Matayo and Julia have decided not to proceed with entering the foster care scheme. Eventually Matayo admitted he was not ready for the challenge and felt he was not as committed to it as Julia. Julia in turn felt that Matayo would not be able to give her the support she would need for a foster care placement to be successful.

Although painful, it was evidence that the process was working when potential foster carers were turned down or chose to withdraw despite the immediate and urgent need for carers.

Preparation

During the assessment and selection process the team considered possible children waiting to be fostered and which may be most suited to a particular family. This is sometimes referred to as 'matching'. There were obvious factors to bear in mind such as age, religious or tribal background, siblings, the child's stated preferences, location and space available. In addition, personality and temperament as well as specific concerns should be aired and agreement reached about the most suitable placement.

The child prepares

The preparation process for each child varied. It was embodied in the aims and programme at Tudabujja, the halfway home. There were specific areas to address in relation to family life depending on the experience of the child to date. We learned it is wrong to assume that a child who has had a negative experience of home and family life will automatically let go of their fears and projections when relating to a new family. The halfway home concept allows a child to broaden his or her experience of 'family' prior to foster care and enter the next part of his journey with a positive and hopeful outlook. Each child was encouraged to consider the way families operate and the 'rules of the home', the unspoken expectations and ways of behaving that ensure family life goes on. Even though families review and adjust these at times, they generally remain in place and a foster child should be prepared and encouraged to respect their new family's ways of doing things.

The family prepares

The areas covered during assessment shed light on what needed to be prioritised with the family during the preparation period. Relations with the community or wider family may need strengthening as was the case with Lydia and Rashid:

> Lydia and Rashid were motivated and devoted parents to their own four children. Initial visits by Solomon went extremely well and we hoped the foster placement could begin within a month. A serious delay occurred after it was reported that Rashid had been hit by a relative. We were 'summoned' to meet with elders in the village who alerted us to division in the family. Although Rashid had not converted to Christianity from Islam, he was being accused of weakening the faith of the family by fostering a boy from a Christian background. In reality the issue was as much to do with land as faith but a series of meetings were held and agreements drawn up and the situation very closely monitored. It reminded us of the importance of the wider family and community. We may need to explain what foster care is all about to a bigger audience than just the immediate family and to win the trust and support of leaders, neighbours and friends to make it work.

Other areas considered included practical arrangements to do with space, sleeping arrangements, finance, schooling or domestic chores in the home and compound. Again, agreement was needed to ensure as smooth a transition as possible. Supervision in the home is an issue especially with younger children. One lad had become so used to constant company both on the street and for seven months at the halfway home that he found being alone between school and his foster mother coming home almost unbearable. Things went awry until this was identified and addressed.

Siblings were included in as much of the process as possible. They too experienced a lot of change. In our experience they were excited at times and anxious at others. One challenge for social workers was to evaluate how realistic siblings' expectations were and whether they were ready to adapt if expectations were not met. Matching should try to incorporate shared interests but adjustment will be inevitable as space, time, toys and attention all have to be shared with another person. There may be considerable gaps in educational ability, and difference in the life experience of the child being fostered and the natural child may be a source of strain or at least concern to the parents.

Meeting other carers

In addition to meetings with social workers and home visits it was possible for potential carers to meet with existing foster carers. We invited some potential carers to all or part of training days and on some occasions arranged for foster carers to come with us on home visits. Long term carers were encouraged to be honest and open about challenges, surprises and disappointments as well as the rewards, joys and benefits of fostering.

Contact visits

There was usually a mixture of fear and intense excitement whenever a child visited his prospective family for the first time. Time and energy at the halfway home focussed on preparing for life in a family and community and residents and care workers shared anticipation and joy when a child left and returned from initial visits to a family. Introductions were handled by the social worker who would normally stay for an hour.

The frequency and length of visits varied according to the needs of both family and child but typically the length of visits increased. In between visits parents and siblings were urged to keep talking about the effect of having a new child in the family. Social workers were encouraged to time visits so that children were back from school and could tell them about the visit and their feelings towards the process.

Placement

The following section of the introductory literature referred to the day a child was welcomed into a new family:

> By the time you welcome a young person into your home you will know about them and will have had them to visit and possibly to stay for several nights prior to the final preparation period. You may feel anxious about the forthcoming change and possible disruption to your lifestyle and routines. Your children may also be feeling concerned about the impact on them.

Of course there was often excitement and the family would have been assured of the valuable contribution they were about to make. By being realistic at the outset we pre-empted the need for honesty at later stages. As well as the immense privilege of welcoming a new child into the home, privacy would be invaded, property may be misused or borrowed and there would be a price to pay in terms of hassle and energy. Behaviour may be unpredictable. There aren't enough pages here for the stories foster carers shared with us once they realised their experiences were normal.

The welcome and first few weeks were critical and workers should have been available to visit daily if necessary. Some teething problems were easily solved but entering a family may remind a child of what he or she has been through in the past. Even when they had experienced abuse or neglect, some children still felt the pain of separation from their birth families. We discovered that some issues addressed earlier on in the process re-surfaced during periods of transition or at particular times later on. Foster carers were encouraged to depersonalise their response to outbursts of anger or when a child said he didn't want to be part of the family.

We introduced the concept of 'rules of the home' and in the early days of a placement, carers were encouraged to make these clear in positive ways while being flexible as the child adjusts. By watching the behaviour and conduct of others in the household almost all children fostered understood what the expectations were and rose to the challenge to taking part. In Uganda 80% of the population still depend on agriculture for their livelihood. All children are expected to participate in chores and farming activities and this had to extend to children being fostered. It reinforced why we included training in sustainable farming in the programme at the halfway home.

Training and support

Foster families recruited to look after former street children in Uganda are some of my greatest heroes. They have had to learn patience, understanding and tolerance. Our commitment to them included an offer to train and support them for as long as was felt necessary. In early stages of transition this was especially important but many long term carers continued to participate in three foster care support days and a foster care residential retreat each year.

Foster care support days and retreat

These were special occasions that provided a forum for training but also enabled us to thank and encourage carers who had invariably made big sacrifices. Transport was provided and venues were spacious and welcoming. The support days and retreat were open to all foster carers, children being fostered and one sibling (usually the closest in age to the child being fostered). Towards the end of our time in Uganda that meant around a hundred people coming together with a common purpose – to strengthen family life.

At times children and parents had separate programmes and at others they came together for joint training through games and activities. Meals were great occasions and would often be followed by light-hearted games. The power of play was clearly evident as children and their foster parents laughed with and at each other and entered in to the spirit of competitions and challenges. Skills were taught by social work staff and visiting experts and there was plenty of time and space for group and individual work to address specific issues and to share recent experience and acquired wisdom. Experienced carers took part in leading groups and discussions. The programme was designed with particular needs and individuals in mind but the following are examples of areas covered:

- Listening to children and young people.
- Integration and identity.
- Stigma and challenges at school.
- Culture and heritage.
- Sex, sexuality and relationships.
- Managing difficult behaviour.
- HIV and AIDS related issues.
- Relating to the wider community.
- Sharing the vision of foster care.
- Fostering and family life skills.

Carers and workers learnt from each other and this list grew over time. It was several years before we encountered head on some of the heightened issues of identity that face children in long term foster care or adoption during adolescence. Issues related to infant attachment or the impact of separation and trauma can emerge at later stages. At one retreat three carers each shared how they had to deal with outbursts of anger unlike any they had experienced with their own children. There was a shared determination to avoid placement breakdown and by hearing how peers had coped, carers felt better equipped to work through difficult times.

Primarily through the events mentioned above but also through exchange visits we aimed to develop a community of carers who would strengthen and encourage each other. Positive feedback from support days normally highlighted the benefits of meeting with and learning from 'peers' in foster care.

Support

The critically important issue of practical or financial support given by the project has been left to the final section of this chapter. It is often the first thing I am asked about by people considering or initiating foster care programmes but was often the *last* thing we mentioned to potential carers. Finance featured at the end of our introductory literature. Of course it is hugely important in settings where many people can barely support their own children let alone someone else's.

> *Our priority was to find carers motivated by genuine concern, envisioned and able to appreciate that, irrespective of support given, there would be demands and sacrifices. The risks of foster care being seen or treated as an income-generating activity are great but we aimed to reduce the risk by delaying and minimising reference to financial support.*

Our initial commitment was to guarantee that the costs of fostering a child would be met by the project. In other words, the family would be no worse off as a result of this brave step. In practise that meant regular support with feeding. Support from the World Food Programme enabled us to provide each family with food equal to the extra amount needed. It required considerable coordination and effort but reduced the need for cash payments. School fees and requirements were met by the project and in some cases extra support given to enable the nearest sibling to attend school.

As understanding and relationships grew other possibilities emerged for empowering the family to raise their level of income so they could absorb the costs of an additional child. The question of whether we should, as a matter of course, offer micro-finance or loans arose but we were strongly advised against setting precedents that could hinder us taking in to account variance in ability and motivation. The donor mentioned above actively encouraged us to build a 'community of carers' but guided our thinking around the dangers of confusing a social work relationship with an economic or financial one. The obligations and expectations were different and could have created unnecessary tension. Despite that, we allowed room for creative thinking and the possibility of support to strengthen family businesses or to enable specific ventures to take off.

> Anthony, Rogers and Charles were found by older street boys living in a burnt out car. Their mother had died leaving them in the care of a grandmother who also died just six weeks later. For two months they fended for themselves in the room rented by their grandmother but eventually made the journey to Kampala thinking they may find relatives or assistance there. They were six, eight and ten years old. Against all odds a couple were found who were willing to care for them. What was even more incredible was that Maria and Sam had no less than five children already! The process was formally recognised by the district court and the family showed great determination to fully integrate all three boys. Once settled, the issue of strengthening the family's economic situation was explored. Sam was skilled in building and had been stock piling bricks from his earnings in order to build his own house which would mean an end to rent payments. The project drew up an agreement with him which included generous payment in bricks in return for assistance with construction at the halfway home.

Other examples included help with a small restaurant, expansion of livestock, licensing of businesses and cultivation of land. Instead of offering fixed grants after a certain period of time we aimed to demonstrate a genuine and fair commitment to each family according to their needs and capacity.

Social work support continued to be available throughout the placement. After the transition period, the length, frequency and nature of visits were reviewed. It was usually the social worker who had overseen the assessment and preparation that continued to work with the whole family.

Outcomes and success

The outcomes of a foster care placement may be easier to define and measure than those for resettling children with their own families. However, breakdown of a placement should not imply 'failure'. It may be temporary or lead to other possibilities. The child may have experienced love and security for the first time and may have grown and developed beyond what he would have done had foster care not been attempted. We were caught unprepared for the onslaught of adolescence with some boys fostered at the age of ten or eleven. Five years later it became evident that we had not prepared carers adequately for their changing role and some placements broke down.

> Jeremiah's story continued. When he reached sixteen we had to find alternative accommodation for him. His foster mother's health had deteriorated at a time when his behaviour was becoming difficult to manage. They continued to enjoy seeing each other and the relationship resembled one we might experience with a grandparent.

The foster care team monitored very closely each child's experience of school. It was important for schools to be aware of the situation and of the wider support available should problems arise. Social workers contacted and visited schools and were asked to arbitrate if behaviour was causing concern. One school had not had a single occurrence of theft until one of the lads fostered joined. In his first term there were five incidents! The social worker and parents worked closely with the school to help him tackle this behaviour and the underlying issues surrounding it. Despite these initial challenges we were consistently amazed at both the academic and social performances of children fostered. Although it is well documented that children in long term foster care or adoption often achieve higher than average exam results, the impact foster families were having struck us afresh at the end of every term.

Contact with natural families was encouraged once circumstances and motives for wanting to meet had been verified. There were times when a significant change had taken place in the birth family. On one occasion a child's sister contacted us with news that their mother was seriously sick and had asked to see her son. A series of visits were arranged prior to her death and both foster family and child were grateful for the opportunity to reconnect at such a sensitive time. A few children who had been fostered for a long time began to explore the possibility of reconnecting or at least receiving more information about their family.

One of the most exciting outcomes was a celebration of new identity. When a child declared he was no longer 'a Tiger' we rejoiced with him. When a child declined an offer to visit the halfway home we rejoiced and eventually stopped planning such visits. When a foster family told us 'This boy is now one of us – he is truly a Mayanja' we rejoiced with them. When we heard that the project had not been contacted when a fostered child was ill and the family had dealt with it, we rejoiced. That was what it was all about. The ties were being loosened. To be possessive about children we are entrusted to work with for a while flies in the face of a transitional approach.

Summary

I was and remain passionate about foster care – and specifically seeing it develop in Uganda. It kept me focussed and energised. Foster care must be defined clearly. The background to launching a 'foster care scheme' was given in order to highlight: the rationale for it, the importance of relating it to the legal framework, the strategic value of finding partners, the need to continually review and learn, accessing resources and the existence of networks. The scheme itself focussed on the components of a long process including recruitment, assessment and selection, preparation, placement, training, support, outcomes and success.

My first insight into fostering was as a social work student on placement in an area of urban deprivation. It fascinated me then as it does now. One assignment was to visit a couple in their home who had been approved to foster what were then referred to, somewhat callously, as 'hard-to-place' children. The team had an individual in mind and my task was, in the course of conversation, to make them fully aware of the extraordinary challenges they would face. As each piece of potentially alarming information was shared, their excitement at the prospect of fostering the child grew! They had fostered in the past and knew what to expect. I was humbled by their spirit and sacrifice. They knew that even though it may seem a thankless task, it has the power to restore dignity and release potential. The same was true of the community of foster carers in Uganda.

Setting up or improving foster care services may seem daunting but I hope what has been shared will inspire practitioners and decision makers to take bold steps to make the vision of a home for every child a reality.

Conclusion to Chapter 4

I have attempted to communicate an understanding of the meaning and implications of a transitional approach to working with street children. In isolation from working holistically, relationally, in a child-centred and professional way, some of that meaning is lost.

A transitional approach implies journeying with street children for a while and empowering them to move on. It necessitates placing or positioning residential care as a possible part of that journey rather than a destination. Like any journey, the transition of street children should have a beginning and an end. Like any journey, it should be planned but there will be unforeseen hazards and delays so flexibility and creative thinking will be needed at times. Transitions involve change and uncertainty, letting go of some things and embracing others. Vision and confidence is needed to get through transition and I hope that what has been shared will enable others to envision and build confidence in street children preparing for change.

5   A Child-centred Approach

Introduction

To ascertain a street child's best interests we must remain child-centred and this chapter considers what that means in practice. It explores involving street children, communicating clearly with them, removing assumptions and pre-conceived definitions of 'the problem' of street children and ensuring street children fully understand processes and options. Direct work with street children that is child-centred is time-consuming and challenging and entails:

> . . . developing multiple, age, gender and culturally appropriate methods for ascertaining their wishes and feelings, and understanding the meaning of their experiences to them.
>
> DoH, 2000

The following claim that a child-centred approach to development is the foundation of all nation building cannot be taken lightly:

> Taking a child-centred approach is essential to breaking cycles of denial that restrict children's capabilities and potential. It is the only way to address patterns of ill health, inadequate nutrition and the limitations of no or poor education. It is the foundation of all nation building.
>
> UNICEF – Child Centred Development

Street children are amongst those whose capabilities and potential have been restricted so people working with them should grasp what being child-centred is all about. It is as relevant to development at a macro socio-economic level as it is to effective grassroots social work practice. Working with street children means: getting involved in complex situations, confronting wider issues and meeting individuals other than the child herself. Situations, issues and individuals demand our attention as can policies, procedures and donor demands. They are important but not 'central' to the social work process. In other words, they should influence but not dictate the way we work or priorities and targets we set. One of the most significant pieces of childcare legislation ever passed in the UK recognised the harm that can be done when attention is diverted away from the child:

> . . . the overarching framework for assessing the needs of children and young people under the Children Act 1989 stresses the importance of being and remaining 'child centred'. Attention should not be diverted towards other issues, or other individuals, especially in complex situations where the **primary purpose of the task is to ascertain the child's or young person's best interests.**
>
> Smith, 2008 (my emphasis)

There were undoubtedly times when we assumed we were 'child-centred' when we weren't, both during pioneering years and once established. External and internal pressures may have led to cutting corners in our social work practice for the sake of producing impressive numbers or succumbing to media pressure to speed up the work or produce tangible results fast. It is easier and less time consuming to be formulaic in response rather than genuinely seeking and responding to a child's wishes and feelings. Being child-centred entailed: shaping thinking amongst staff team members, implementing and constantly reviewing practical measures to prevent them from becoming tokenistic. We will consider child-centred thinking first.

Child-centred thinking

Five inter-relating concepts are central to child-centred thinking in social work with young people. They are childhood, development, participation, empowerment and choice.

Childhood and development

I hope that people reading this will be working with or considering working with street children in different countries around the world. I am convinced there is common ground amongst street child workers globally, value in sharing experience even when differences are revealed and universally relevant principles and concerns. However 'Child social work and practice do not operate in a vacuum, but in particular social and historical contexts' (Kirton, 2009).

Even within one society there will be an evolving understanding of childhood and development. A child-centred approach should involve examining our own understanding of childhood and its significance. Our own experience and assumptions will affect our thinking and how we judge others so we should take time to consider them. Cultural 'norms' exist in regard to expectations to be met by children, discipline of children, relationships between children and adults, behaviour in public and private and degrees of understanding by children. If we are working cross-culturally it is doubly important to appreciate that such norms exist and try and build an understanding of them by being open and perceptive. One of the benefits of an increasingly diverse culture in the UK is that more literature is available than ever before concerning effective social work across cultures. Working in Africa meant tuning into a collective or interdependent orientation rather than a western orientation which is predominantly individualist or independent. This impacts identity and community, family dynamics, childcare practice, parenting styles and socialization. Of course not all people within a culture behave in exactly the same way and the dangers of stereotyping and generalising are real and should be fiercely guarded against.

Childhood is a reality but what is it? Is it just a 'stage' of psychological development? This view has been challenged by many who view it as intrinsically valuable irrespective of culture or time:

> James (in Theorising Childhood, 1998) emphasises the need to see children as 'beings' (the fully fledged social actors they are in the present) rather than 'becomings' (the adults they may be in the future).

Kirton, 2009

Even though there are huge variations in practices and expectations relating to childhood, the inherent value of childhood is similarly emphasised by the President of Compassion International. We used this quote in staff team development and displayed it on the team office wall as a poignant reminder:

Too many of us tend to treat childhood as a preamble to actual life, a vulnerable period of time merely to be survived in order to get on with the real business of being valid, contributing members of the human family. This is the mindset that causes us to talk of children as 'tomorrow's world' . . . As noble as that sounds it is all about pushing off the value of children to the Realm of Someday — Someday they will add value.

Stafford, 2005

Development is, of course, an aspect of childhood. In the West we consider Jean Piaget and Erik Erikson as champions of child development but many writers have adapted or developed their concepts since. They identified stages of development — linguistic, social, moral, cognitive and physical — and attributed them to certain age ranges to establish developmental milestones. They were pioneers in psychological development theory and being familiar with their work and models may be a good starting point even if the social and cultural environment you are working in is not the same as theirs.

It is widely accepted that few children and young people follow a neat or uniform developmental pathway. There are many variables and development in one aspect does not imply development in others. In other words, physical development does not imply emotional maturity nor vice versa. Whilst having a secure knowledge base about growth and change in all areas we need to view each street child as a unique individual developing in his own way. It is generally agreed that all cultures feature key transitions as children and young people age or mature. These may involve changes in living arrangements, means of survival or expectations or contributing to the needs of the community. Smith describes these as 'global aspects of youth and development'. They provide the contexts in which biological, social and psychological changes occur.

In summary — child-centred thought embraces the notion of childhood as having huge cultural and social variance but inherent value. Street child workers should critically review and reflect upon their own childhood in order to understand at a deeper level the childhood of those in the dominant culture in which they are working and more specifically of those who have been forced to spend most or all of it on the street. Workers should be able to answer the following question of street children — How does their experience of childhood relate to or diverge from what they would have experienced in mainstream society?

Child-centred thinking includes an awareness of development. Many theories of development are Eurocentric but can provide a starting point for considering development within your own cultural context and current 'norms'. Bearing in mind that development is rarely linear and uniform, street child work demands an understanding of the transitions and changes a child will experience and his or her response to them. Understanding the context or 'systems' within which a child grows and develops is sometimes described as an 'ecological perspective'. It is explored in *Cross Cultural Child Development for Social Workers* (Robinson, 2007) which relates attachment theory, identity, cognitive development, communication and socialisation to cultural perspectives and social work practice. In Uganda and in Ethiopia it was essential to learn about cultural norms in relation to these and other aspects of childhood and development. There were tribal and regional variations too which were brought to our attention by fellow team members and street children themselves.

Participation, empowerment and choice

In every professional relationship there is a power dynamic and the one at the heart of this book – between worker and street child – is no exception. The art of social work is to ensure that the power dynamic is constructive and pure. Participation and choice are two concepts closely related to power and both have the potential to *em*power.

Sadly, 'child participation' has become another catch-phrase in child care services generally and in the development world especially. At a pan-Africa conference in Nairobi hosted by the Consortium For Street Children (CSC) in 2001, country representatives were asked to present a situational analysis. Many delegates felt duty-bound to include a section on 'child participation' – invariably tagged on at the end and delivered with fading energy. It was a relief to us all when a conference leader insisted those remaining abandoned the apparently obligatory 'child participation' sections of their reports. No one was belittling the concept but acknowledging that it had lost the significance and meaning it deserved.

Participation is linked firmly to power and choice in the following succinct definition:

> *Forms of involvement where people play a more active part, have greater choice, exercise more power and contribute significantly to decision-making and management.*

> Adams, 2008

In *The Art of Youth Work* Kerry Young locates participation at the heart of all that youth work aims to achieve. She suggests the purpose of working with young people is essentially about moral philosophising – about meaning and finding answers to the question, 'How should I live?' To do that, purpose should be made explicit, understanding should be clarified and consent to engage should be conscious and informed. Some of these themes were raised earlier and are inextricably linked to participation:

> *Participation in youth work is more than simply taking part or having a say. Participation involves a process of conscious, critical self-reflection that can only be entered into voluntarily.*

> Young, 2009

I use the language of journeying with street children largely because it implies a mutual experience – doing something *with* rather than *to* them. There is reciprocity in the relationship between 'helper' and 'helped' which is a concept brilliantly advanced by Brazilian educational philosopher Paulo Freire. His thinking about the teacher being a learner and the learner being a teacher can be extended or applied to the street child worker and the street child or homeless youth. He wrote in his classic text *Pedagogy Of The Oppressed*:

> *One cannot expect positive results from an educational or political action program which fails to respect the particular view of the world held by the people. Such a program constitutes cultural invasion, good intentions notwithstanding.*

> Freire, 1986

Extending or applying this means that work with street children cannot expect positive results if it fails to respect the particular view of the world held by street children themselves. Genuine participation of street children means that their view is fully heard and they are empowered to understand choices and make decisions. Freire warns that, *'to alienate humans from their own decision making is to change them into objects'*.

It has been a privilege to work with and learn from individuals and organisations which aim to manifest this thinking in their work. Dr Jember Teferra has spearheaded community development, physical upgrading and primary healthcare through IHA-UDP in Addis Ababa. It embraces a 'bottom-up' approach to development which responds to the felt needs of the poor and empowers the poor to teach the poor. In summary it:

> *. . . looks upon its work with the poorest of the poor as being holistic and integrated primarily because the approach is participatory and the community is viewed as both the agent and beneficiary of the development project.*

> Teferra, 2001

Umthombo in South Africa aspires to demonstrate genuine participation. Its thinking is summed up:

> *Umthombo has borrowed from Steve Biko's Black Consciousness thinking and Paulo Freire's conscientisation ideas to develop what is termed Street-child Consciousness. Street-child Consciousness is a philosophy that empowers street children and former street children to overcome the false message from society and re-envision themselves as full human beings. Instead of seeing themselves as rubbish, they learn to see themselves as survivors and people with knowledge and an ability to change things for other street children who are still on the street.*

> Hewitt, T. (undated)

These are two examples in which street children experience the kind of critical self-review mentioned above and which we should study and emulate if we intend to go beyond tokenistic participation. There are numerous ways of classifying types of 'participation'. Hart (1992) adapted a ladder of participation to work with children and young people. It has eight 'rungs' with manipulation (which is non-participatory) at the bottom and shared decision-making at the top. It helps to review and measure what we label 'participation' using such a framework.

Participation implies and increases empowerment which Adams describes as:

The capacity of individuals, groups and/or communities to take control of their circumstances, exercise power and achieve their own goals and the process by which they are able to help themselves and others to maximise the quality of their lives.

Adams, 2008

To be truly empowering, participative measures and activities must be appropriate for a child's age, development, level of ability, interests and desires. It is not always fair to expect participation on our terms or to put someone in a position of responsibility when these considerations have not been taken into account. We have a responsibility to equip children with the tools to participate. Street life is such that some street children (not all) develop skills and confidence, sharp insight and the ability to find solutions. Others need strengthening and encouraging in these areas or in areas such as self discipline, confidence and assertiveness, resolving conflict and trustworthiness. In working with children at risk and their families, there may be a tension between empowerment and protection which must be acknowledged and worked with rather than ignored. In practical terms, what happens when empowering a street child with the ability to choose results in a choice to return to an abusive situation? Or should we empower children to remain on the street knowing that the risk of abuse by others or themselves is extremely high? If we do not take into account ability, age and understanding of consequences but focus solely on a child's stated desire I fear we are not being either child-centred or empowering.

After working with young people in a privileged environment, I concluded that there is a thin line between essentially positive notions of being *'spoilt for choice'* and the negative connotation of being *'spoilt* **by** *choice'*. In high income countries there is a risk of overwhelming children and young people with too much choice. For street children the opposite is true. Many street children feel that circumstances control them rather than the other way round – that things happen to them. This perception and the daily struggle to survive eliminate any concept of planning ahead or tackling a range of options. Closely related to participation and empowerment is the aim of increasing choices and the ability to make them. This is easier to state than do with children who, through repeated disappointment or perceived failure, may have little motivation to think beyond the immediate future. We encountered this time and time again and it was indicative of the paralysing effect of what Seligman called 'learned helplessness'. One example was Isma.

Isma was offered an incredible opportunity. He had spent 12 of his 16 years on the street and had never been to school. Street kids gave him the nickname Kiyenje, which means cockroach, because he was short and rarely washed. Since we first met him his confidence had grown and despite severe learning difficulties he responded well to individual attention from teachers. After treating Isma, a local doctor heard about his background and offered him an apprenticeship at the restaurant she owned. We helped him prepare for a meeting which was not a formal interview but an opportunity for Isma to present himself and so 'earn' the apprenticeship. His behaviour at the meeting was alarming. Isma crouched and cowered in the corner and covered his face with his arms. He refused to respond to any questions asked by the owner and became tearful and scared. Isma had behaved in a similar way in remand homes and court. It seemed he could not distinguish between the owner and authority figures he suspected or assumed were against him.

Street child workers reading this will have similar accounts which remind and challenge us to go beyond creating and presenting choices to street children. We need to equip and enable them to make decisions and to understand the consequences of each option, in ways that are appropriate to each individual.

Child-centred practice

This section attempts to relate thinking to practice. How a child-centred approach manifests itself in programme design and implementation will of course vary from one context to the next. I will share some of the ways we aimed, not always successfully, to be child-centred to generate ideas or affirm what is already being done.

Child-centred counselling

The aims and process of counselling street children were shaped by a desire to enable participation, critical self-review and empowerment. In fact counselling that does not empower is not counselling! Those involved in formal counselling were regularly challenged to ask themselves the following questions:

- How does our understanding of being 'child centred' affect our practise as counsellors?
- What do we *really* listen for?
- How do we hear the views and wishes of the child?
- How do we use counselling to enable informed decisions?
- Are we sure that the child we are with understands the consequences of choices and decisions?
- How do we avoid being over-directive?
- How do we tailor programmes to allow for individuality, personality, varying levels of development?

In Chapter 3 we considered many aspects of the counselling process in the section on 'Hearing and Listening'. Much of the material assumes a commitment to a child-centred approach. The questions above probe deeper into both the style and content of our counselling. The answers should reveal the extent to which style and content are truly child-centred and where we need to adapt or develop in order to make them so. They are the kind of questions that can guide thinking and discussion either in the supervision of key workers or during 'baraza' style meetings as outlined in Chapter 2.

In addition the thinking and awareness of childhood and development should influence attitude, priorities and the direction of our counselling. It should provide us with a lens to view each individual child and their response to our interaction and guide our planning to make counselling meaningful and appropriate.

Measuring impact

The five concepts discussed above – childhood, development, participation, empowerment and choice – provide benchmarks for measuring the impact of our work on each individual child. Tracking change with these benchmarks may not be as straightforward as measuring tangible outcomes such as school attendance or numbers in foster placement but are of equal value. As with any qualitative change or measure they require narrative reporting which can be time consuming in comparison to ticking boxes or plotting on charts. Both are essential for different reasons and I regret that we paid far too little attention to documenting and distributing the findings of such 'impact tracking'. This was especially true during the years of pioneering and innovating new aspects of the programme. The hours worked, energy spent and need for spontaneous action were far beyond anything I've experienced before or since so there was rarely time left in the day to chart progress made or write up developments. With hindsight I would urge those starting out to make time – or slow down if necessary – in order to reflect and record both quantitative and qualitative changes in the lives of street children in your care. More recently, impact tracking has been prioritised and formalised. An organisation, which designed an impact-tracking database, advised us to create one which accurately and fully reflected the nature of the work being done. That advice is especially relevant if work with street children is 'child-centred' and the purpose of measuring impact is primarily to improve service delivery.

Forums

Open and honest communication was encouraged from the outset at the Tigers Football Club and continued as the organisation grew and developed. Participation is a spectrum from tokenism to shared decision making and there were times when, intentionally or otherwise, we were nearer one end of the spectrum than the other. An organisation committed to a child-centred approach will allocate time and space and create safe environment for groups and individuals to speak and be heard about general concerns, specific issues, designing, planning and delivering services. For us that meant organising:

- *Pitch-side Meetings* – after every training session the football coach was joined by other staff team members for sharing news and information, hearing from the lads and responding to concerns.
- *Feeding Programme* – the open feeding programme included time prior to the meal for group discussion and feedback. After the first few years, we failed to sustain this pattern and underestimated the importance of using it to connect with street children we didn't see at other times. During and after the meal staff members were encouraged to engage with new arrivals on the street as well as longer term members.
- *Site-specific 'community meetings'* – these were opportunities for those at the refuge, school boys hostel or halfway home to air views and contribute to the running and future of the centre.

- *START Days* – these were held three times a year for all boys at school, at vocational training centres or setting up small businesses. They served multiple purposes but always incorporated opportunity for small and large group discussions and opportunity for feedback and suggestions.

Growing leaders

One of the most exciting yet challenging aspects of all youth work is identifying and supporting young people into responsible leadership. That was true for our work in Uganda although it was often frustrating and never easy. The point was made earlier that development and maturity is not as linear or uniform as theorists may have implied. Social maturity may not develop in parallel to emotional development. For these reasons, it may not always be in the best interest of an individual young person to offer him positions of responsibility. It may conflict with or hinder their choices or decisions, needs or plans. The stories behind these statements reveal how we learnt some of these lessons the hard way.

The Junior Management Team (JMT) was a group of six former street children who had been through the programme and demonstrated leadership potential in various ways. They had gained the respect of both staff and fellow street children. Each individual was allocated an area of responsibility and the group met on a monthly basis with the director and usually one other staff team member. I came away from those meetings energised and surprised although I should have anticipated the outcome. Whether we were discussing specific individuals or issues, general strategy and direction or plans to develop one or more areas of work, the insights of this particular group of individuals were invaluable. Formalising their role and introducing more defined tasks, badges and improved time-keeping proved frustrating and time-consuming itself. For some individuals, participation on the JMT seemed to empower but in fact delayed or hindered their progress towards greater independence. The tension between the value of participation and being transitional in our approach had to be resolved. We limited the length of time someone was on the JMT and aimed to replace one member with a new member every six months to maintain momentum through the JMT and into the community. One example is mentioned in the following quote after a JMT meeting:

> Abdulaziz has been an outstanding member of the JMT and we publicly thanked him. Since realising that he will be the next to 'graduate' from it he has asked to train at Lubwama Agricultural Insititute and the farm manager has agreed to prepare him for this. He is aware of a plot of land belonging to his family that he is entitled to dig but if there is a problem, he intends to apply to one of many new commercial flower farms in his district.

A child-centred approach is one which takes the views of children seriously and the JMT is just one example of identifying and empowering those with leadership potential which enabled us to hear and honour those views.

Summary

The quote from UNICEF in the introduction to this chapter has far-reaching implications for those working with street and marginalised children. Being centred on the child rather than other issues or agendas means thinking in a certain way and the inter-related concepts of childhood, development, participation, empowerment and choice were introduced in order to direct our thinking and attitudes accordingly.

What aspiring to be child-centred meant in practice (in our context and at a specific time) was described to illustrate what it may mean for you. Child centred practice was demonstrated in child-centred counselling, measuring impact, creating and maintaining forums for open and honest communication and growing leaders.

6 A Professional Approach

Introduction

The purpose of this chapter is to consider becoming and being 'professional' in direct work with street children. The previous four chapters inferred that working with street children is demanding and requires skill and determination, so this chapter should come as no surprise. Professionalism must permeate all other aspects of an approach to bring about lasting transformation and excellence in our work. What it means to 'be professional' in the charity sector and in the field of social work are vast topics. Although they can't be tackled here, it is important to be aware of and acknowledge the difficulties of defining 'professionalism' and the debates about professionalisation processes in relatively new and emerging professions.

The need for this chapter is crucial because of the prevalence of non professional activity in both charity and social work sectors. Both sectors stem from voluntary movements to bring about social or personal change and the spirit of 'voluntarism' remains a huge aspect of both. When we talk of the charity world or field of social work we refer to a spectrum of hobby style activity and groups at one end to formalised organisations and highly skilled technical experts at the other. Work amongst street children is no exception and there are literally hundreds of groups, teams, individuals and agencies on every part of the spectrum described.

In some cases the spectrum represents a pathway of growth and development and this was true in our situation. From the outset there was a vision for a better world, a willingness to give up time and energy on a voluntary basis, a group of friends and supporters and increasingly strong relationships with those the founders sought to serve. All those elements were foundational to the emergence of a social work organisation that was recognised as effective in fulfilling its objectives, had credibility with users, peers and the wider community, adhered to values, codes and integrity and prioritised the development of people as skilled practitioners – in other words it moved along the pathway towards being 'professional'. Those processes happened in countries in which we were delivering services to street children ahead of countries which were sending money and resources. In those countries where we relied heavily on goodwill and voluntary support for many years.

Thinking professionally

Even in contexts where there are few, if any, trained social workers or courses available, it is possible to first think professionally and then act professionally in working with street children.

Being strategic, selective and focussed

Most directors and founders of street child agencies will have stories of those offering to help or of streams of volunteers coming to do their bit in response to the plight of and challenges faced by homeless children.

An American lady arrived at our gates one morning and as usual children gathered around the new arrival. The first cause for concern came when she began handing out sweets and encouraging the lads to call her 'Mummy Leanne'. In due course a meeting was arranged away from the Clubhouse. Leanne peered at me intensely behind enormous pink-rimmed glasses as she reported a series of dreams that had led to her conviction that she was to work with street children in Uganda and more specifically at our project. She believed this had come from God. The dreams culminated in a scene of her standing in the middle of a busy street surrounded by African children clambering for her attention. She had no specific skills or training or experience but just wanted to do whatever would bring hope and help to the children of her dream.

Needless to say we did not receive the same divine instruction to immediately appoint this lady but I share this incident with you to illustrate some of the pressure those running street child agencies may face. It was one of literally hundreds of offers of 'help' over the years and a professional approach meant scrutinising each offer and firmly prioritising the development of a national staff team. The following incident was also one of many.

It was a shock this morning when a group of 14 UK students appeared at the Clubhouse. They were all female (apart from one) between 17 and 23 years old. We'd sent a message to the organisation arranging their programme explaining that because we worked exclusively with lads and focussed on equipping national staff it would not be possible to host a team. The message didn't get through or wasn't taken seriously! As I was ferrying half the group across the city in the van, the conversation in the back disturbed me. The students were comparing what different agencies offered in terms of trips to Africa and commenting as if browsing through holiday brochures. 'I would've gone with (another agency) but they only offered Zambia and it was one day less but cost more – this is loads better'.

The gap year and summer expedition 'industry' is growing. Some organisations are extremely careful about its effect on long-term work. They adhere to codes of best practice in regard to selection, training, support and assignments. Others are less discerning and emphasise the warm welcome given and life-changing impact on those visiting to justify sending more and more people each year.

I am touching on this issue because it relates to thinking and acting professionally. The key question surrounding volunteers and visits, particularly for those in projects within international agencies is, 'Who is serving who?' To genuinely serve the needs and encourage professionalism of teams and individuals on the frontline, frontline leaders should set the agenda and have control of visits and volunteers. I worked alongside street child workers exhausted not because of the direct work itself but because of yet another group or individual from overseas. The level of supervision and added workload created are far greater than one might expect. Those in leadership should be aware that in some cultures it is unacceptable to refuse a visitor. I have known local managers politely agree to visits from the UK knowing that it is not necessarily in the best interests of the national staff or the children they are seeking to serve. We avoided being UK-centric by ensuring visits only occurred once frontline teams had answered the following questions:

- *What is the purpose of the visit?* These included, sharing specific skills, to train team members, to represent and report back to long-term supporting churches.
- *Does the visit serve the needs of the team or children?*
- *Are there designated staff members willing, able and available to take responsibility for volunteers assigned to their department?*
- *Is the timing and length of visit right for the frontline team?* For example, periods of change for the team sometimes made visits difficult or inappropriate.
- *How do those coming understand their visit or voluntary work?* A spirit of learning was essential and those who came expecting to 'change the world' were often the least effective.

We did not always get it right but were increasingly careful to introduce criteria which confirmed a desire to think and act professionally. As a result we welcomed teams and individual volunteers who fulfilled those criteria and had a positive impact during their time with us. Two football coaches from youth academies in the UK, special needs teachers, a dentist, graphic designers and artists, clergy, builders and medics all contributed in a way that truly helped rather than hindered the long-term relational work.

I have considered an issue that affects almost all street child agencies in order to introduce and illustrate the following aspects of thinking professionally:

- *Be strategic* For us that meant defining and sticking to our aims of developing strong national staff teams.
- *Be selective* The questions listed above prompted us to think deeply about offers of support and discern carefully whether to accept them or not.
- *Be focussed* It was tempting sometimes to open the floodgates to overseas volunteers especially when it seemed cheaper and easier than building a team locally. Instead we aimed for sustainability and effectiveness by recruiting, training, supporting, equipping and strengthening national staff.

Values, principles and ethics

All social work with street children involves working relationships and the use of power. Our attitude towards them determines our level of professionalism. There is an ethical use of power which is key to professional social work and should be defined and applied to each context, reviewed and reflected upon. The values of the family, of the community and each individual underpin aspects of the overall approach described in this book. They have been explored in other chapters. The values and principles of culture and heritage, communication, teamwork, respect and integrity are also foundational to a professional approach.

I led an organisation that was faith-based and in our literature we stated that, 'many staff team members are empowered and motivated by their Christian faith'. We held beliefs that strengthened what we did and determined the way we did it. That included aiming for excellence in order to fulfil a Biblical mandate to care for the most vulnerable members of society in a sacrificial way. At the official launch of our new brand 'Retrak' in London, I was approached by the then director of the Consortium For Street Children who was impressed and encouraged by what he had seen and heard. He said to me:

> I am intrigued by the way you seem to exemplify best practice and yet at the same time you are strongly faith-based. Perhaps you could teach other agencies who don't seem to manage to be both.

I explained that from the outset we aimed to be non-manipulative, non-judgemental and non-discriminatory in our approach. There might be greater pressures and reasons for faith-based agencies to manipulate, judge and discriminate – and many are perceived to be doing so – but I am convinced that faith can enhance our ability to uphold core social work values and deepen our impact as a result.

Personal development and responsibility

The need for a spirit of learning was emphasised above and this must extend to workers who claim to be professional in their approach. The need to learn and grow can be misunderstood as weakness in some contexts. During interviews in Uganda, our terminology had to change to emphasise challenges and learning opportunities rather than gaps, weaknesses or needs to assess a candidate's self-awareness and readiness to change or grow. A commitment to increase understanding through training and relating theory to practice is essential.

In addition to this, workers needed to grasp the need for codes of conduct and be willing to develop appropriate language and behaviour that reflect a professional attitude. That may involve establishing boundaries, understanding and managing the tension between confidentiality and safeguarding, managing expectations by honouring appointments and time-keeping and committing to collaborate with other workers. Our attitude to and understanding of the significance of these determine how they manifest in daily practice.

Acting professionally

An organisation is only as strong as its people and this section falls into two sections both essentially to do with personnel and their ability to deliver a professional approach to working with street children.

Core social work competencies

The Board I worked for asked me to identify the core social work competencies that are essential for working professionally with street children. The purpose was not to insist every key worker had to demonstrate all of them but that within the team these skills were represented. Most are explained and incorporated in other chapters. Of course there will be variations according to context but this list may provide a starting point for reference:

- *Ability to form professional relationships* with individuals, families and communities.
- *Awareness of relevant theory and research, methodologies and legal framework.*
- *Ability to understand and respond to:*
  - *Childhood development*
  - *Trauma*
  - *Indicators and impact of abuse before and on the street*
  - *Status and self-esteem*
  - *Anger and self-control*
  - *Drug misuse and addictive behaviour*
  - *Sexual development, identity and relationships*
  - *Criminal activity and conflict with the law*
  - *Specific aspects of individual street children's experiences*
- *Assessment skills to identify strengths and needs, gather information and measure effectiveness.*
- *Generic and specialist counselling skills* including the ability to interview, negotiate, form working partnerships and facilitate participation. I appreciate that where resources are limited, the scope for referrals and collaboration may be restricted. However, it is important to acknowledge individual or team limitations in certain areas. There were times when we did not have the necessary expertise, and sharing the need led to contact being made with experts we had not previously been aware of.
- *Ability to plan and implement appropriate interventions with children* including the ability to plan and work towards 'closure' effectively.
- *Management of facilities and centres* in a way that reflects the social work ethos and aims of the organisation.
- *Ability in social skills training, anger management and conflict resolution.*
- *Oral and written communication.*

Human resource development

Getting the right people in place is of supreme importance in any organisation aiming to be professional in its approach to working with street children. It is one of the most demanding, sensitive and never-ending features of any effective social work agency. There is only space here to highlight some of the principles learned through both positive and negative experience:

- When staff members are over-stretched and demands are growing, it is tempting to accept anyone and to create a role around them rather than the other way round. Although more challenging, the reverse was undoubtedly more effective – identifying needs and roles that fit the aims and objectives and then finding the right person. Organisational fit is crucial in a relational setting and it is worth waiting for the right person.
- Motivation was as important as skills or technical expertise. We were criticised at times for being over selective but our strategy was to find people with sufficient qualifications and experience or who demonstrated commitment to go on developing necessary skills. For those

who showed real potential in social work we tried to facilitate opportunities for further study. In one case that meant a highly skilled social worker went on to attain a degree in social work.
- Internal support is discussed below but during recruitment processes we tried to establish what external support would be available to frontline workers. National staff often told us of the stigma attached to working with street children and the extra pressure that put on them. To redress that we encouraged them to inform families, neighbours, church leaders and friends about their work and ask for their support emotionally, practically and spiritually.

Teamwork and team building were touched upon earlier in regard to being holistic and creating a staff team stronger than the sum of its individuals. A professional approach seeks to ensure individuals are well supported through effective performance management and review, supervision and training. The growing professionalism of the team were noted by many who made return visits:

> I was astounded at how much more confident and professional the staff team has become since my last visit. They have developed the ability to make a difference in young people's lives.

> Start, 2001

Such encouragements motivated us but there was always more we could and should have done. Key lessons learnt included:

- Staff team members needed to be clear they were part of a bigger picture and that their role in fulfilling the vision was highly valued. Staff team days and retreats were planned with this in mind.
- In the Ugandan context, the education system emphasised learning by repetition and recall. We wanted and developed a team that didn't simply recite core values and the five 'pillars' that together form the approach described in this book but lived and breathed them in their daily lives and work. It was a priority to ground values, principles and the five pillars in experience by using them to question, develop and review work done.
- I am frequently asked about terms and conditions for staff and most notably their salaries. Even though we were a UK registered organisation we could not possibly compete with some international donor agencies and multi-national organisations whose pay scales bore little relation to the costs of living. The concept of 'market value' lost meaning and relevance when an agency paid drivers double what we were eventually able to afford for our most highly qualified social workers. At the other end of the spectrum, skilled and motivated staff members at other agencies were paid very little but produced excellent work at grassroots level. It was essential that staff had a sense of vocation and pride in their work and were duly rewarded and relieved of anxiety about income. We analysed reasonable costs of living and pay-scales of mainstream employers. Our teacher could have been employed by a top state-run school. We decided to pay him twice what he would have been paid there. For our Project Nurse we doubled the salary of a registered nurse in the main government hospital.

Medical insurance and savings schemes were introduced and staff sent their children to decent schools and saved to buy land. It is a challenging and sensitive area and we were criticised by some for paying too much and by others for paying too little. Yet for a decade we had an extraordinary level of staff retention and continuity which is vital for an effective social work organisation. Despite the huge demands and the need to make sacrifices, many team members felt compelled to work hard and remained loyal for many years in order to see lives transformed.

Summary

This chapter has highlighted what a professional approach means both in our thinking and attitudes and our practice. It has focussed on the delivery of effective social work rather than organisational development, structures, protocols and procedures, governance and accountability. Of course those elements are critically important but should be designed and positioned to truly serve the needs of frontline workers. Why? In order to prevent an organisation from losing its 'cutting edge', watering down its impact or more positively to enable and nurture a professional approach to direct work with street children.

7 Getting Started

Introduction

The purpose of this chapter is to encourage and inspire new initiatives and to give practical guidance to those starting out. You may wonder why this chapter comes so late in the book. My intention was to first define, describe and explore an approach to working with street children. I hope that as a result, some are impelled to go forward and devote time and energy to implement or commission new initiatives with street children. I also hope that some are deterred from doing so as they have been challenged to reconsider what is involved. Positioning this chapter at the beginning of the book may have given the *wrong* message that working for street children is feasible or appropriate for everyone and anyone moved to do so.

The main features of how operations began in Uganda can be found dispersed through preceding chapters. It is not presented as historical narrative but is used to accentuate lessons learnt as we translated theory into practice to fulfil a vision. Instead of repeating what's been said, this chapter focuses on the implementation of a new work in Ethiopia – or, more accurately, the process leading to that implementation. It provides another illustration of launching a new initiative.

In Kenya, instead of implementing work ourselves, we decided for various reasons, to work through partnerships with existing local projects. That is the preferred mode of operations for many agencies. Although the process of selecting, initiating and establishing effective partnerships is beyond the scope of this book, key elements listed at the end of the chapter may be adapted accordingly.

Branching out

As far back as 1996, some of us imagined a day when we would venture into other African countries. It sounded daft at the time but we genuinely believed that if the dream became reality it would be crazy not to use that experience elsewhere. Street child workers and agencies face constant demands for new, quicker 'solutions' to the phenomenon of street children but I firmly believe there are no short cuts to lasting, transformation of individuals and society. What is needed is for responses that have proved to be effective to increase and improve. In ten years time if there are *more* projects doing *better* work amongst street children as a result of agencies and projects sharing experience and strengthening each other, the impact on statistics and social trends will be huge.

Between 2002 and 2005, the Retrak Board made strategic decisions to support the expansion of work to other countries. Before doing so a process of visits, lengthy discussions, formal meetings, concept papers and collective soul-searching had to happen. We needed to be certain of our identity, of the risks involved and that there was a genuine role for us in other African cities.

The first exploratory visit to Addis Ababa was made in August 2003 in response to an invitation and encouragement from organisations already there – GOAL Ethiopia and Serving In Mission (SIM). After hearing about our work and, in the case of GOAL, visiting the work in Kampala, personnel from both suggested we investigate the possibility of developing work among street children in Ethiopia.

The Board asked for clarity around the aims of an initial visit and these were agreed as follows:

- To gather accurate information about:
  - the current situation regarding street children within Addis Ababa.
  - intervention and service provision available from government and non-government sectors.
  - perceived gaps in service provision (geographical, approaches, target groups etc).
  - the social, administrative, political context in Addis and Ethiopia generally.
- To make contact and build links with key players in work amongst street children.
- To explore possibilities for formal and informal partnerships with relevant organisations.
- To assess the feasibility of the model forming the basis of work in Uganda being applied to and used in Addis Ababa.

A full report of the visit was presented to the Board including key facts and statistics about the context and in-depth feedback from meetings with eight existing NGOs. The findings were both quantitative and qualitative as we gathered historical, social and political information as well as views and opinions from a wide range of people. Issues relating to street children and key socio-cultural, political and legal differences between Ugandan and Ethiopian contexts were noted which would inform our thinking and planning.

A document proposing a way forward was drafted and taken to the Board for further discussion, amendment and approval. After intense dialogue, discussion and reflection at a retreat in October 2003, the Board, management team and other key players agreed that Retrak:

- Has a unique philosophy and approach that should be shared with others to maximise our impact.
- Has something to contribute alongside existing efforts to address the enormous and possibly overwhelming street child situation in Addis Ababa.
- Should encourage networking and partnership at all levels as it has done in Kampala and that this is relevant to the situation in Addis Ababa.
- Proceeds with caution to investigate the prospect of working in Ethiopia without in any way jeopardising existing work or hindering further development in Uganda.

Time frames were reviewed and the need to create fresh avenues of support emphasised.

Considerable effort went into forming partnerships and managing the expectations of both organisations and individuals. At this stage, care was taken to prevent a sense of rush and a five year plan comprising of research, networking and planning, training and preparation, feasibility study and needs assessment, and legalisation followed by a pilot phase and review was proposed. Operations actually began in 2007 – a year earlier than anticipated.

In April 2004, eight months after the first visit, another visit was made to Ethiopia with objectives set in the light of all that had been agreed upon. The initial intention was to pursue one particular partnership but shortly before leaving the need to explore other possibilities became clear. Revised aims were:

- To explore further opportunities for collaboration and partnership within Addis Ababa or nationally.
- To meet with leaders of potential partner organisations and churches.
- To clarify and expand upon understanding with an established agency in regard to affiliate status for our team leader.
- To gather more information on legalities and procedures regarding NGO registration, work/resident permits, operational and project agreements.
- To gain more detail concerning practicalities of living and working in Addis Ababa.

Important information and understanding was reached about the political framework and requirements for legalisation. Poignant differences between Uganda and Ethiopia would make life easier in some ways and much harder in others. We went ahead aware of these. The summary findings concerned practicalities and procedures, scope for strategic partnerships, the need for and offer of support for key personnel and the need to accept the bureaucratic hurdles which would necessitate building a presence in stages. More concrete possibilities for collaboration with agencies and networks emerged.

By the time of a third visit in November 2004, preparations could be made to pave the way for Retrak to send someone to carry out a full feasibility study and needs assessment in 2005. The person mandated had lived and breathed Retrak for three years and had over twelve years experience in eastern and central Africa. The Board was certain that even in a very different context, the core values and unique strategic approach could be implemented once findings confirmed there was a niche for Retrak to deliver services. The team leader would first spend an intense period studying Amharic. The main findings of the third visit concerned practicalities, entry visas, registration, accommodation, costs, insurance and health services. A modest budget of £10,500 was set for the following year and since then a new and effective work has been established.

Key questions and concerns

The description above highlights a number of considerations when attempting to initiate new work among street children. Expansion was in response to a belief that we should use what had been learned and in response to an invitation. Key questions to consider are:

- Are you responding to a felt need in or invitation to the community or city which you may initiate work in? It adds validity to your intention if you have been invited to explore possibilities.
- What have you discovered about the political, social, cultural and religious context?
- What are pertinent cultural, tribal or linguistic issues?

- What is your understanding of the legal framework and legalisation or registration processes?
- What are the specific issues relating to street children and what are commonly held beliefs about them?
- Have you established exactly who is doing what and where? The feasibility study that followed the process outlined included meetings with staff from 75 NGOs in Addis Ababa.
- Are there definite gaps in service provision? There may be geographical areas beyond the reach of existing work or particular services or approaches not yet being offered.
- Have you clarified what you may be able to offer in this context and that there is a need for it or a 'niche' for your kind of organisation or project?
- Are you committed to building relationships with those already engaged in work with street children?
- Have you identified risks and the way to manage them? In potentially volatile settings we had to identify, manage and review risks including those relating to political systems, changes in government policy, threats to street children, media coverage and reputational risk, staffing issues, child safeguarding and financial or resource management.

For agencies working through partners, the above list can be adapted for selecting partners and clarifying the nature, purpose and possible risks of specific agreements. Other organisations' experiences of initiating new work can be found in publications referred to at the end of the book. No two contexts are the same and organisations differ as much as individuals. However, there are principles and lessons to be learnt from others' experience. In Ethiopia we were able to avoid repeating mistakes in Uganda by reflecting carefully on what we had learnt and in both countries we listened intently to stories of innovation in other parts of the world.

Summary

Motives and support for initiating new work need to be established. A clear invitation to do so adds legitimacy and value for those entering a new country or city. The following are key elements to getting started:

- *Needs assessment and feasibility* to establish the scale and nature of a problem, a gap analysis in regard to service provision and the scope for involvement.
- *Research and relationship building* to identify and map out all that is being done, to build bridges with community, authorities, other NGOs and potential partners, to learn from others' experience and avoid working in isolation.
- *Understanding legal frameworks and structures* and the need to meet requirements. Registration processes are lengthy and arduous. At times the bureaucracy was overwhelming especially if corruption is prevalent. For Ethiopian registration we endured parallel processes in London and Addis Ababa doubling up forms, interviews and payments over a period of a year. It was costly and hard but essential to get established.
- *Defining and managing resources and expectations* including finances, personnel, time and facilities. Expectations should be realistic and tangible measures set within a strategy for

specific areas or projects. Although some argue the adage of 'acting locally and thinking globally' is dated, I maintain its value in helping pioneers of new ventures retain perspective on all they are doing.

- *Analysing risk*, which is an inevitable feature of new ventures. No two projects are the same but it is vital to design a framework to look at and manage risk. If the organisation already has operations elsewhere there may be a need to manage risks to existing work. There may be risks to credibility and reputation. Risks can be resource related, to do with political context or staffing. A starting point is to draw up a list of 'what if . . .?' questions and to assess the scale of impact and likelihood of specific occurrences. If potential impact and likelihood are both high, then measures to reduce them should be taken to mitigate risk to the work and by implication, to street children themselves.

8   A Platform Created

Introduction

We are not to simply bandage the wounds of victims beneath the wheels of injustice, but we are to drive a spoke into the wheel itself.

Dietrich Bonhoeffer

The vision behind this book is of a world in which every child has dignity and opportunity and no child has to live on the street. The aim is to inspire and equip those working directly with children dependent on the street for survival, with passionate spirit and professional skills in equal measure. By improving our service delivery in the way described we inevitably create a dilemma. What do we do with the insights and experience gained to influence those in positions of power to act on behalf of the children we are working with? How do we put a 'spoke into the wheel of injustice' that permits children to live without care and protection? We cannot and should not contain ourselves.

The approach described in this book became the background and foundation of a powerful story that needed to be told. In commercial language we had a product that demanded profile. The same is or will be true of others privileged to work amongst some of the most vulnerable and yet most resourceful children in the world. The experience gained forms a platform from which to speak on behalf of those whose voices are unheard, to act against injustices that lead to children seeking survival and solace on city streets and to raise awareness and support for work being done. This chapter briefly examines the inter-related themes I am referring to: advocacy, prevention and funding. Those who work directly with street children have unique responsibilities relating to all three and each area merits a chapter or book of its own.

Advocacy

Advocacy is pleading for change or promoting a cause. It involves advancing ideas within decision making circles, highlighting issues that demand change and taking action to bring it about. We have explored the concept of empowerment as a key element of effective relational work with street children and an outcome of this will be *self*-advocacy. However, this section concerns advocacy on behalf of those who are not 'voiceless' but who are being ignored or misrepresented.

The experiences and conclusions shared are personal and flawed but offer an insight or starting point to reflect on your situation and opportunities to shape and influence thinking and policy in regard to street children. At times we missed chances, made errors and ignored risks. Despite all of that we were listened to and respected locally and nationally. Our opinion and expertise were sought by those in authority. Part of the reason for that was a willingness to get involved and work with government agencies from the inside. I watched closely as those who insisted on shouting abuse from the sidelines were literally sidelined. They lost credibility and influence and so any chance of channelling their anger to produce change was lost.

Over time it became clear that there are 'zones of influence' which could be applied to different parts of an organisation such as ours. Some advocacy *had* to happen at a local level as it could only be effective through personal relationships, networks and contacts, local and immediate media opportunity and direct influence on local authorities. There are daily opportunities to shape opinion and we have already noted sensitising communities at the point of reconciling children with their families, holding community meetings at the drop in centre and submitting letters, articles and interviews to the local press on a regular basis. Some issues may call for advocacy at a higher level in addition to local pressure. The following examples from my time in Uganda are of one-off or less frequent opportunities and what we learned through them:

Marching on the streets

Rallies and marches are popular in many parts of the world and Uganda is no exception. On three occasions we took to the streets. The Inter-NGO Forum, described in Chapter 2, was asked to participate – and ended up organising – one such march to officially launch Best Practice Guidelines for Working With Street Children. It culminated in a celebration in one of the city squares in which each NGO was allowed to exhibit its work and crafts produced by street and former street children. Children themselves played a huge role in the day and spoke alongside senior politicians and leaders from the main stage. Performances were given and there was a heavy TV and radio presence. A key aim was to redress the imbalance of media portrayal of street children and the myths and assumptions that were spread as a result. Literature, banners, speeches and interviews all reflected this aim. Other marches were held for specific events such as the Day of the African Child. These provide internationally recognised occasions to raise profile and awareness. Some questions asked and comments made by highest-ranking officials revealed serious gaps in knowledge and understanding or a refusal to confront the real reasons for children being forced to live on the street.

Speaking out on children's rights

One harrowing episode followed reports of street children being recruited for military purposes in a war across the country's border. Eighteen children told us they had either refused to go or physically escaped from training. I made these findings known at a meeting entitled 'Hearing the Voice of the Child'. The meeting's aim was to explore violations of child rights so it seemed a safe environment to do so. A media frenzy ensued which led to me being summoned to meet government officials. I was sternly warned with the words, "Williams – of course there is freedom of speech here but from now on you speak to us first"! I agreed, with certain conditions, that one child should testify about his experience. He accurately answered every probing question to the amazement of those gathered. Reports of recruitments stopped so the outcome was a good one but in the meantime a media campaign and threats from one particular source made for an uncertain and unnerving time. Lessons were learned with hindsight. Although it was right to speak out and act, a proper assessment to manage and mitigate risks to individuals and the organisation should have been made with the board.

Seeking justice

I was called into the austere city morgue to identify the body of Hamid who had been shot three times in the head and stomach. Hamid was a bright and cheerful lad who, against the odds, had set up a charcoal stove making business. Reports came in that he had seized an opportunity to snatch a lady's mobile phone while riding the bike he had diligently saved up for. A chase broke out, he was forced into a ditch by the side of the road and he threw the phone back to the owner. After doing so a law enforcement officer (not trained police) ordered his shooting. We gathered as much information as we could and discovered there were almost 40 people who witnessed the event. At the same time as arranging a burial, tracing relatives and supporting his friends, we embarked on a process to seek justice. In short we failed despite hours of meetings, interviews, escorting witnesses to give statements, seeking legal advice and liaising with regional authorities. Eventually we were informed that the director of public prosecutions had ruled that officers involved had acted 'in the course of duty'.

Shortly afterwards I met Gary Haugen, founder of the International Justice Mission (IJM) firstly in Kampala and later in their Washington offices where I discussed the case. Haugen addresses the church with a challenge to seek justice but emphasises the different roles there are in that process. He cites the need for country and culture experts, public justice professionals, international business people, storytellers and communicators including those in media and journalism to play their part. Of frontline workers which would include those working directly with street children he says:

> These workers must share . . . the stories of oppression and abuse that they hear and see.
>
> Haugen, 2009

He outlines a three step process of developing eyes and ears to see and hear about injustice, to aid the victims of abuse by helping them articulate their story and to be 'responsible stewards' by telling the story. The IJM has a referral process for reporting cases of abuse and violation of rights and an increasing number of legal professionals ready to respond. Although it was impossible to re-open the case of Hamid, IJM have investigated other incidents of street child deaths and brought perpetrators to justice. We learnt the importance of defining roles and collaboration if advocacy is to be effective.

Government initiatives

It is impossible in one paragraph to fully describe a two year process of working with the government to influence and reshape thinking and planning in regard to the rounding up of street children. In summary, we were invited as the representing agency of the Inter NGO Forum with two or three others to respond to a proposal to remove children from the streets and accommodate them in Kampiringisa, an institution designated for capital offenders. Unlike previous similar operations, which were knee-jirk responses to the arrival of one or more dignitaries, the intention was for a collaborated and long-term programme utilising funds available as a result of debt relief. It became apparent very early on that if we refused to cooperate we would no longer be invited to participate but that the programme would proceed anyway. Hence a decision to get involved which led to 84 hours of meetings with senior government officials and an agreement to support social work processes through the programme that were in the 'best interests of the child'. We were careful not to condone forced removal of children and refused to be present at or part of the transfer of children from the streets to the centre. The Commissioner for Children and Youth readily agreed that to do so would jeopardise our working relationships with the children once there. The programme at Kampiringisa continued for many years as anticipated and the NGOs that worked with the government despite ideological differences have been able to maintain a presence there. They run specified activities and services whilst trying to ensure children are reunited with relatives or referred to other agencies. It was an example of advocacy which involved collaboration without compromise to create change from the inside. It was only possible because of strong working relationships forged over many years.

The four examples given involved those working directly with street children although not exclusively. Others commissioned research and shared the findings so that experiences were incorporated into reports and documents which could influence at a higher level. Advocacy needs to happen at different levels to influence without jeopardising the immediate social work being done. That was one reason for building a presence regionally in Nairobi where there was scope for voicing concerns, networking, region-wide research and engaging with higher levels of authority. Similarly, there are networks and alliances in regions that can add leverage in a way that individual agencies cannot and I would encourage all NGOs and projects to seek and support such collaboration.

On an international level, networks such as the Consortium for Street Children UK, European Federation for Street Children, the 180° Alliance, Child Rights Information Network and others gather information and urge governments and inter-governmental bodies to change policy or bring pressure on those violating children's rights. They rely on projects around the world to ensure relevant and experience-based campaigns.

Prevention

> *Prevention is problematic because it involves stopping an event from happening (the street involvement of a child) therefore its success is difficult to prove.*
>
> Plan International, 2011

It is reassuring to read prevention described as 'problematic' because it has caused me real concern over the years. It is another word that trips off the tongue in development circles. Hardly a week went by when we weren't asked about our plans to prevent children migrating to the street. Of course we all want to find easy solutions and of course there is truth in the adage 'prevention is better than cure'. However, an emphasis on prevention generates the risk of diverting attention from the immediate need for rescue and rehabilitation. Both words are regarded by some as outdated as they imply the helped are passive in the case of 'rescue' and somehow to blame in the case of 'rehabilitation'. Yet they highlight the need for immediate intervention of some sort and shortly after arriving in Uganda we defined much of our work as 'crisis intervention' with all the complexity that implies. There is an urgency about all that is described in this book. In the mid-nineties the demands for prevention programmes from some donors were so great that one organisation with 14 years experience in direct work with street children abandoned their rehabilitation and reintegration programmes altogether. Attention and resources were diverted away from direct work with street children as a result.

Although there are patterns and trends, there are as many reasons for children coming to the street as there are street children. Assuming 'prevention' can be an add-on or alternative to the kind of programmes described denies the complexity and diversity of factors leading to a child depending on the street for survival. Two risks have been identified: diverting attention and resources and ignoring the complexity of reasons children arrive on the street.

A serious question also arises 'how can we be *certain* that what we are doing really is 'prevention'? Families in the same adverse conditions do not *all* marginalise children or break down or lead chaotic lives. Prevention programmes may in fact be community development programmes which are worthy in themselves but are not necessarily preventing migration. Yet I do believe in prevention and that individuals who have worked with street children over many years have unique insights at a local level into behaviour, attitudes, circumstances and pressures that together may lead a child to the street. As with advocacy there comes a responsibility to use that knowledge to inform and inspire and to review what can be done in a targeted way to prevent a rise in the number of street children. JUCONI's work in Latin America is often cited as exemplary in this regard. In an overview of the JUCONI model prevention is discussed:

> *Prevention is only cheaper if preventive services (whatever their nature), actually serve children at risk of becoming street children. And here we have a major problem: how do you identify who is actually at risk of becoming a street worker, a market-worker, or a street-living child, and who is not? The JUCONIs have faced this dilemma, and have come to believe that the children most at risk of taking to the streets are the younger siblings of street children, who share community and family situations.*

> Thomas de Benitez, 2001

JUCONI learnt important lessons from early initiatives aiming to prevent children becoming street-workers:

> *Our conclusion when we assessed the value of JUCONI's 'community-extension' services was that we may well have had a significantly positive impact on women's formal participation in local communities, but we had not had an impact on preventing children*

from taking to street-work. So, in terms of impact on the street-working child population, our prevention strategy had turned out to be a cost with no identifiable benefit, making our prevention work not cheaper, but in fact 'expensive'.

Thomas de Benitez, 2001

By targeting children that share the same family environments as those currently living on the street they have developed a model that is likely to prevent children coming to the street. Latin America is a different context to East Africa but the principle of carefully targeting work we label as 'prevention' is universal. I have not attempted to explore macro-economic or political causes of migration to urban areas but needless to say prevention has to be tackled at those levels too. A practitioner's role as story-teller has been discussed. By offering accurate, truthful information to families and communities and by raising awareness of the problems faced by children on the streets we may add to the prevention process.

Funding

It is beyond the purpose of this book to explore fundraising in relation to street child work. However, two areas often raised by those pioneering new work are donor relations and child sponsorship.

Donor relations and communication

Relations with donors are inevitable and have already been discussed. Whether individuals, churches, schools, companies or trusts there is a trend towards partnership in all its forms and need to grow relationships between donors and beneficiaries. Trust and accountability are critical and all new or young organisations need to develop and adjust as demands increase. Over a ten year period our annual income grew from around £10,000 to almost £500,000. Subsequently, demands grew and new demands arose from different types of donor. Our first multi-year funding in 2001 has been described in relation to foster care as an especially positive experience. The foundation was committed to mutual learning as much as to targets and statistics. We received initial funding from two major institutional donors paving the way for larger grants and allowing us to evolve into an agency that met reporting requirements within donor-designed frameworks without being donor-led. Support from individuals and churches, both locally and abroad, was smaller in financial terms but invaluable in terms of commitment and encouragement. Some churches maintained support for twelve years — four times longer than many corporate or institutional donors.

Accountability to such non-institutional donors is equally important. Regular communication should offer truthful, consistent and accurate information. It is alarming to read what some agencies assert in literature or on the Internet. One agency claims to resettle more street children each year than actually exist in the city where it is located. It is tempting to inflate figures or embellish facts but providing exact information to donors whether individuals or international agencies will add a stamp of integrity to an organisation which will serve it and its beneficiaries in the long term. We found that when supporters felt engaged and valued, well informed and treated with respect they would continue and increase levels of support given.

Child sponsorship

One of the most powerful fund-raising strategies must surely be child sponsorship. It is an area we were frequently asked about and many agencies have asked for guidance about. I have concerns about child sponsorship ideologically and practically but particularly in relation to street children. On a general level concerns are risk-related and I know some organisations have managed and mitigated these risks carefully. In brief, the main risks are that children are reduced to commodity status, donors are elevated to saviour status and that programmes may be unsustainable when faced with some of the challenges agencies face.

Situations and reports I witnessed prompted scepticism about sponsorship: children with sponsors in five countries and leaders diverting funds for their own use, children writing to sponsors reporting abuse by local staff and asking for money to be sent directly to another address, projects receiving sponsorship for children who had in fact died and families disguising actual circumstances to claim eligibility for sponsorship. I met a social worker from Ethiopia whose family had not spoken to him for 18 years. They had treated him with contempt since the day he became a sponsored child.

I am not sure how widespread such practices or effects are. They may not exist in other parts of the world. Some large agencies have gone to great lengths to tackle them but an awareness of such risks and dangers is important if embarking on child sponsorship. Even if such risks were mitigated, I felt child sponsorship was inappropriate for our particular situation. Street children's lives are often chaotic and unpredictable and our approach was non-formulaic and flexible. By contrast, children sponsored are usually on fixed programmes with predictable outcomes and sponsors are assured of continuity and uniformity.

Summary

Experience, knowledge and insight from working with street children form a platform or foundation from which we can raise awareness, plead for change, tackle root causes and increase support for our endeavours. In short, advocacy, prevention and funding are themes we are inevitably challenged to consider.

In relation to *advocacy* the main points were: to define it, show that it's possible to work within systems and structures to effect change, and that zones or levels of influence should be identified from the local to the international. Advocacy involves awareness raising and redressing imbalances in media or public opinion, suggests that collaboration need not imply compromise and shows that risks should be assessed and managed in relation to advocacy by practitioners.

Regarding *prevention* I highlighted the issues over defining and measuring prevention, and danger of diverting attention and resources away from direct work with street children. To be meaningful, prevention needs to target specific groups and that our role as storytellers contributes to the process of preventing children coming to city streets.

Brief comments on *funding* and support demonstrated that: forming and building partnerships are a growing feature of fundraising, trust and accountability are essential and as an organisation grows demands will increase and change in regard to trust and accountability. Adaptability is vital to respond positively to donor-designed frameworks without compromising effective work or being 'donor-led'. Long-term or indefinite commitment from at least some donors was recommended. Finally, concerns were expressed, risks highlighted and caution urged in regard to child sponsorship and its suitability to raise funds for street child organisations.

9 Now I See My Future . . .

I used metaphors of a fight and a journey to begin exploring an approach to working with street children. Returning to those metaphors, there were many times I contemplated desertion, looked for an escape route or wished for an easier road to travel. Meeting and hearing individuals working with street children in other parts of the world, convinces me I was not alone. We have discussed motivation and vision, values and objectives but these alone are not enough to keep people on the frontline or to maintain momentum during the toughest sections of the journey.

There is a clock tower at a crossroads in the centre of Kampala. Coming from home, the road to the left led to Entebbe Airport. The road straight ahead led to the base of our work with street children. At times, when I knew what lay ahead or of pressures from other angles, I would have gladly turned left. Why didn't I? It certainly wasn't common sense. It wasn't courage or confidence. Even compassion wavered at times. It must have been a conviction that something **was** happening in the lives of our travelling companions. Perhaps it was the memories and experiences of tangible transformation within street children who had transitioned from despair to hope – children like Richard or Fred.

Richard's sporting ability was noticed by our coach and he was invited to train with Tigers FC. Initially, he didn't meet the criteria for joining as he lived with his mother in the heart of the slum and had received sponsorship from a Catholic priest to attend school. However, his situation was precarious. Richard's mother was unable to walk having lost the use of both legs. Instead, she wore flip-flops (known locally as 'slippers') on her hands and managed to manoeuvre by dragging her withered legs along the floor. They shared one room in a mud shack. Richard's nickname meant 'son of war' and it transpired that his father was a soldier and he was the result of an abusive relationship during a time of conflict. He and his mother came to Kampala when he was nine years old and begged together. Shortly after we met Richard, his mother became seriously ill with repeated bouts of TB and Richard faithfully carried her to the far side of the city for treatment. She died and we enabled Richard to arrange a funeral. He was by then captain of Tigers FC and was supported to train as a chef. He found employment in a fast food restaurant but fell out of favour with managers when he protested about the way asylum seekers were being treated. Richard tested positive for HIV shortly after we spotted some indications of the syndrome. His determination was extraordinary and was noticed by the clinic prescribing anti retro viral treatment. They were impressed and offered him a job which he excelled at. We were reunited in Uganda recently, when he proudly presented his son Benjamin – a healthy one year old – and told me he had 'dared to dream the impossible'.

The story outlined includes uncertainty, disappointment, sadness, frustration and joy. The journey called for flexibility and creativity, patience, trust and determination by Richard and all of us travelling with him. It reminds us that measuring success is not an exact science but that lasting transformation is possible. Access to treatment and his strength and commitment enabled Richard to live positively with HIV.

Kapapa means 'titch' and was the name given to Fred when he arrived on the street at the age of four. He was one of the first four boys supported by Retrak to attend school. He had no living relatives but never grumbled. He always offered to help and encouraged both staff and children with smiles and positive comments. After completing six years of school Fred's health deteriorated rapidly due to a kidney deficiency. The medical team worked tirelessly to relieve pain and enable him to regain strength but eventually he had to be hospitalised. It was an agonising time. With no dialysis machine available in Kampala, the only option was to send him to Nairobi which, despite complications of securing a passport and the need to raise funds, we planned to do. However, before we could proceed, the strain on Kapapa's body and heart became too severe and he died. That afternoon I had sat with him. He began to weep, beckoned me to his side and pleaded, 'Uncle, just take me home'. In the heat of the moment, I thought he wanted to disclose new information so asked him what he meant. He smiled gently and whispered 'Tigers Club – of course'. It struck me forcefully that, for some street children, working with them meant nothing less than becoming and being 'home'.

During the initial stages of imagining this book, I recorded 40 more stories, from Kampala alone, that I hoped to include but have not been able to. Each one represents a real person, actual circumstances and relationships. The number is tiny compared to the thousands whose lives are being affected by individuals I have met and learnt from, working in Asia, Eastern Europe and South America and throughout Africa.

The scale and complexity of problems faced by street children are overwhelming at times and the approach explored in this book confirms that there were and are no quick-fix solutions. Seeking them is a futile exercise. Instead we should strive to build on what has already been done – to improve existing services, to initiate new work, to celebrate best practice and to challenge decision makers and those in authority to empower the most vulnerable members of society. My prayer is that this book will have contributed in some small way to furthering those aims by encouraging, equipping or envisioning readers. Vision is life-giving as Sam discovered.

Sam drifted onto the street over a period of two years. One tragic death after another within his family meant he lived with an aunt whose new husband resented his presence. Sam was pushed out of the home. He was a strong footballer and energetic team player with a great sense of humour. We supported him through vocational training and to set up a cobbling business. However, deeper transformation had to happen before these efforts would be sustainable. Behind the laughter and apparent confidence were self-doubt and unresolved anger unearthed in counselling and an episode of disturbing behaviour with other lads. The way we responded, in line with the approach described in this book, was critical. In due course, Sam graduated and received tools and a grant, but that wasn't all. While playing in the Baganda clan's football tournament, he was spotted and invited to play for the national team of a neighbouring country! When asked how Retrak had changed his life, he simply replied, 'Now I see my future'.

Sam discovered worth and realised potential but more importantly had a vision. Almost 2600 years ago, a young Hebrew prophet had a vision of a place where God's rule prevailed. It would be a city in which the streets would be full of children – not crying, scavenging or fighting; not cowering, being spat upon or ignored; not frightened, running or struggling to survive – but 'playing'. It's a picture of laughter, growth and discovery, of sharing, relationship and freedom. It's a picture of children protected, peaceful and living life to the full. It's a picture that transcends time and culture. Whatever context you are in, whatever position you fill, role you play or stage of thinking you are at, I hope this book inspires you to seize the opportunity to journey or continue journeying with street children in a way that empowers and liberates.

The streets of the city will be full of children playing.

Bible, Zechariah, 8 v 5

References and Resources

Adams, R. (2008) *Empowerment, Participation & Social Work*. Palgrave Macmillan.

Anderson, J. (2001) *Restoring Children of the Streets*. Action International.

Annan, K. (2010) *Football for Hope*. FIFA from www.fifa.com.

Beeftu, A. (2000) *God Heard the Boy Crying*. Compassion International.

Blatter, J.S. (2010) *Football for Hope*. FIFA from www.fifa.com.

Bowlby, J. (1997) *Attachment and Loss*. (trilogy). Pimlico.

Byrne, I. (1999) *Human Rights of Street and Working Children*. ITDG Publishing.

Cairns, K. (2002) *Attachment, Trauma and Resilience*. BAAF.

Collier, P. (2008) *The Bottom Billion*. Oxford University Press.

Colton, M. and Williams, M. (Eds.) (2006) *Global Perspectives on Foster Family Care*. Russell House Publishing.

Covey, S.R. (1992) *Principle Centred Leadership*. Simon & Schuster.

Covey, S.R. (1998) *The Seven Habits of Highly Effective Families*. Simon & Schuster.

Davies, M. (Ed.) (2008) *Blackwell Companion to Social Work.* 3rd edn. Blackwell Publishing.

Department of Health (2000) *Framework for Assessment of Children in Need*. HMSO.

DfE (2010) *Children Looked After in England Year Ending 31 March 2010*. HMSO.

Ennew, J. (2000) *Street and Working Children: A Guide to Planning*. Save The Children.

Ennew, J. and Swart-Kruger, J. (2003) Introduction: Homes, Places and Spaces in the Construction of Street Children and Street Youth. *Children, Youth & Environments*, 13: 1.

Feeney, T. (2005) *In Best or Vested Interests?* CSC.

Freire P. (1986) *Pedagogy of the Oppressed.* Penguin.

Geldard and Geldard (2007) *Counselling Children.* Sage Publications.

Geldard and Geldard (2009) *Counselling Adolescents.* Sage Publications.

Hart, R. (1992) *Children's Participation*. UNICEF Essay. Int'l. Child Dev.Centre.

Haugen, G. (2009).*Good News About Injustice*. rev. edn. Inter Varsity Press.

Hennessey, R. (2011) *Relationship Skills in Social Work*. Sage Publications.

Hewitt, T. (undated) *Philosophy*. from www.umthombo.org.

Howe, D. (1995) *Attachment Theory for Social Work Practice.* Palgrave Macmillan.

IFSW (2010) *IFSW Review*. on www.ifsw.org.

Janoff-Bulman, R. (1992) *Shattered Assumptions.* The Free Press.

Keirsey, D. and Bates, M. (1984) *Please Understand Me*. 5th edn. Prometheus Nemesis.

Kilbourn, P. (Ed.) (1997) *Street Children: A Guide to Effective Ministry*. World Vision.

Kirton, D. (2009) *Child Social Work Policy and Practice*. Sage Publications.

Laming, Lord (2009) *Protecting Children in England*. HMSO.

Lefevre, M. (2010) *Communicating With Children and Young People*. The Policy Press.

Lule, J. (2006) *The Hidden Wisdom of the Baganda*. Humbolt & Hartmann.

Martin, R. (2010) *Social Work Assessment*. Learning Matters.

Matheson, A. (2010) *In His Image*. Authentic Media.

Mcdonald, P. (2000) *Reaching Children in Need*. Kingsway.

Mcleod, J. (2007) *Counselling Skill*. McGraw Hill.

Mweaigye, D. (2005) Article. *The Roar*. Retrak.

Mwiti, G. (2006) *Child Abuse; Detection, Prevention and Counselling*. Evangel Publishing.

Mwiti, G. (2009) *Crisis and Trauma Counselling*. Evangel Publishing.

Myers Briggs Type Indicator (MBTI) © www.myersbriggs.org

Okitipki, T. and Aymer, C.(Eds.) (2008) *The Art of Social Work Practice*. Russell House Publishing.

Parker, J. (2008) Assessment, Intervention and Review. In Davis, M. (Ed.) *Blackwell Companion to Social Work*.

Perlman, H.H. (1957) *Social Casework: A Problem Solving Process*. Cambridge University Press.

Pitts, J. (1990) *Working with Young Offenders*. BASW.

Plan International and CSC (2011) *Still on the Streets: Still Short of Rights*. Report for UNHRC.

Retrak (2001) *Annual Review*. Retrak.

Robinson, L. (2007) *Cross Cultural Child Development for Social Workers*. Palgrave.

Ruch, G., Turney, D. and Ward, R. (Eds.) (2010) *Relationship-Based Social Work*. Jessica Kingsley.

Ryan, T. and Walker, R. (2007) *Life Story Work*. BAAF.

Sapin, K. (2009) *Essential Skills for Youth Work Practice*. Sage Publications.

Save the Children (2004) *A Last Resort*. International SC Alliance.

Schaffer, R.H. (2004) *Introducing Child Psychology*. Blackwell Publishing.

Smith, J.F. (1949) *Booth the Beloved*. Oxford University Press.

Smith, R. (2008) *Social Work with Young People*. Polity Press.

Sousa, L. and Costa, T. (2010) The Multi-professional Approach. *International Journal of Social Welfare*, 19: 44–54.

Stafford, W. (2005) *Too Small to Ignore*. Waterbrook Press.

Start, A. (2001) *The Roar*. Retrak, Summer.

Teferra, J. (2001) *Entering the World of Poverty: Handbook for Poverty Alleviation*. IHA-UDP. from www.ihaudp.org/academics.

Thomas De Benitez, S. (2001) *What Works in Street Children Programming?* International Youth Foundation.

Thomas De Benitez, S. (2008) *State of the World's Street Children: Violence Report*. ISPCAN.

Tolfree, D. (2003) *Community Based Care for Separated Children*. Save the Children Sweden.

Ucembe, S. (2010) What it Feels Like to Grow Up in a Children's Home. *Daily Nation*, 23 Nov.

UNICEF (undated) *Child-centred Development*. from www.unicef.org/dprk/ced.pdf

UNICEF (undated) *Understanding the Convention on the Rights of the Child*. from www.unicef.org/crc/files.

Wernham, M. (2004) *An Outside Chance – Street Children and juvenile Justice*. Consortium for Street Children.

White, K. (2002) Ideology of Residential Care and Fostering. *NCVCCO Journal* (now *Children England*).

Williams, A. (2002) *Informal Foster Care Scheme Introductory Brochure*. Retrak.
Wright, W.C. (2000) *Relational Leadership.* Paternoster Press.
Young, K. (2009) *The Art of Youth Work.* Russell House Publishing.

Resources

Support agencies and networks

180° Alliance for street children. is a faith-based action network for those working with street children. I commend the resources section, LEARN, which includes practical downloads, toolkits, articles, research, manuals and other publications. Signing up to enable access is a simple process. www.180degreesalliance.org

Better Care Network. exists to facilitate active information exchange and collaboration on the issue of children without adequate family care and advocate for technically sound policy and programmatic action on global, regional, and national levels. Its website offers access to resources and networking. www.crin.org/bcn

Child Rights Information Network. Global children's rights network. www.crin.org

Consortium for Street Children. has an online resources library with articles and publications categorised according to region and theme. Temporary library membership is available. www.streetchildren.org.uk. CSC has recently published a review of literature relating to street children. Thomas de Benitiz (2011).

European Federation for Street Children. European association. www.efsc-eu.org

Fostering Network (UK). Campaigning, support and resources. www.fostering.net

International Federation of Social Workers. Networking and development. www.ifsw.org

International Foster Care Organisation. Promoting family-based solutions. www.ifco.info

International HIV/AIDS Alliance. Information exchange and resources. www.aidsalliance.org

International Justice Mission. Human rights agency with referral process. www.ijm.org

Keeping Children Safe. Coalition providing child protection toolkit. www.keepingchildren safe.org.uk

Oasis Africa. Consultancy and training on trauma. www.oasisafrica.info

Scottish Institute of Residential Child Care. Equipping in regard to residential care. www.sircc. org.uk

Subsitute Familes for Abandoned Children. Training, consultancy, support in foster care. www. sfac.org.uk

Viva Network. Global network of Christian childcare agencies. www.viva.org

Organisations working with street children directly or in partnership with local NGOs

Africa

Dwelling Places	Uganda	www.dwellingplaces.org
IHA-UDP	Ethiopia	www.ihaudp.org
Mkombozi	Tanzania	www.mkombozi.org
Moroccan Children's Trust	Morocco	www.moroccanchildrenstrust.org
Retrak	Uganda, Ethiopia, Kenya	www.retrak.org
Stepping Stones	Nigeria	www.steppingstonesnigeria.org
Street Child Africa	Africa	www.streetchildafrica.org.uk
Umthombo	South Africa	www.umthombo.org

S. America

Happy Child Mission	Brazil	www.happychild.org
Juconi	Mexico, Ecuador	www.juconi.org.mx
Toybox	South America	www.toybox.org

Others

Action International Ministries	Worldwide	www.actioninternational.org
Childhope UK	Africa, Asia, South America	www.childhope.org.uk
Covenant House	USA, Canada, South America	www.covenanthouse.org
GOAL	Worldwide	www.goal.ie
Jubilee Action	Worldwide	www.jubileeaction.co.uk
Oasis Global	Worldwide	www.oasisglobal.org
Railway Children	India, Kenya, Tanzania, UK	www.railwaychildren.org.uk
Street Kids International	Worldwide	www.streetkids.org
StreetInvest	Worldwide	www.streetinvest.org

Toolkits

World Health Organisation toolkits include: *Working With Street Children: A Training Package on Substance Use, Sexual and Reproductive Health and Working With Street Children; Monitoring and Evaluation of a Street Children Project.* Available from www.who.int/substance_abuse/publications

Similarly the **International HIV AIDS Alliance** has an online resource catalogue with 300 publications and toolkits. Many are extremely relevant and useful to street child organisations. Available from www.aidsalliance.org

Tear Fund have produced a series of books under the banner *ROOTS* looking at aspects of project planning and management including child participation. See www.tilz.tearfund.org/Publications/ROOTS

The **Keeping Children Safe Coalition** has developed a toolkit to enable organisations to design and implement child protection. See www.keepingchildrensafe.org.uk for full details.

Education and training

In some countries there are accelerated learning programmes through government or non government agencies to enable children to reintegrate into mainstream education. In Uganda the *Basic Education for Urban Poverty Areas* (BEUPA) was one such initiative.

Oasis Global have developed resources based on experience of establishing and operating successful projects for children. The following may be of particular interest to readers: *Catch up Literacy Programme, Catch up Numeracy Programme, Step by Step* – designed to measure the individual progress of a child at risk, *Vocational Training Best Practice Manual.*
These are available as downloads or to buy from www.oasisglobal.org/shop

Open Schools Worldwide run children at risk programmes in Africa and the Philippines. They include an education programme called *School in a Bag*. Information and sample lessons are at www.openschoolsworldwide.org

Street Kids International street work programme empowers street kids to develop safe and productive ways to earn a living on the street through two trainings, the *Street Business* and *Street Banking* Toolkits. They also specialise in training of trainers. Details and resources are available from www.streetkids.org

Social work skills and counselling

The following books, which also appear as references, are highly commended:

Adams, R. (2008)	Mcleod, J. (2007)
Bowlby, J. (1997)	Mwiti, G. (2006)
Cairns, K. (2002)	Mwiti, G. (2009)
Davies, M. (Ed.) (2008)	Okitipki, T. and Aymer, C. (Eds.) (2008)
Geldard and Geldard (2007)	Robinson, L. (2007)
Geldard and Geldard (2009)	Ruch, G., Turney, D. and Ward, R. (Eds.) (2010)
Hennessey, R. (2011)	Ryan, T. and Walker, R. (2007)
Howe, D. (1995)	Sapin, K. (2009)
Janoff-Bulman, R. (1992)	Smith, R. (2008)
Lefevre, M. (2010)	Young, K. (2009)

BAAF has several excellent publications, in addition to *Life Story Work*, to use in direct work with children. Visit www.baaf.org.uk/bookshop for full details.

SGM Lifewords (The Pavement Project) have a resource for Christian organisations enabling children to share their experiences of trauma. It should be used carefully, following training and within the context of ongoing relational work. Visit www.sgmlifewords.com for full details.

OASIS Africa offers specialised services and training in relation to trauma and responding to it. Tailor made training was provided in collaboration with Retrak for its first regional training event in 2007. Visit www.oasisafrica.info for further information.

Training workers

There are various courses for street child workers advertised on network websites listed and an increasing number of institutions offering specialised training in international social work.

National and regional training is available through individual NGOs and networks. For example, **Juconi Foundation** in Mexico, Ecuador and elsewhere has a *Technical Support Programme* which provides training for smaller NGOs. **Happy Child Mission** in Brazil similarly offers a training programme including a course for Christian social educators. Visit www.juconi.org.mx and www.happychild.org for full details.

Street Invest is committed to equipping and enabling street child workers across the world. Their training initiative *Take Your Shoes Off* has been effective in several African countries and is set to expand. Visit www.streetinvest.org for full details

VIVA runs workshops, mentoring and a quality improvement scheme for Christian organisations under its *Viva Equip* programme. Visit www.viva.org for full details.

Two organisations are referred to in Chapter 4 in relation to play and sport. They are: Play Therapy International. Visit www.playtherapy.org for details and Rights to Play at www.righttoplay.com.

Project planning and management

In addition to the **WHO** and **Tear Fund** toolkits referred to above the **Juconi Foundation** has produced a paper outlining its model entitled *What Works In Street Children Programming*. It is available along with several useful resources as a download from www.childhope.org/learning.

Judith Ennew's *Street and Working Children: A Guide to Planning* published by Save the Children (2000) is one of the standard books for those initiating new work amongst street-connected children and young people.

Books

Butcher, A. (1996) *Street Children*. Authentic Lifestyle.
De Carvalho, S. (2009) *Street Children of Brazil.* Hodder & Stoughton.
Hewitt, T. (1999) *Little Outlaws, Dirty Angels*. Hodder.
Pritchard, T. (2008) *Street Boys*. Harper Element. (about UK gang culture)
Roper, M. (2006) *Street Girls.* Authentic Lifestyle.

Films

Salaam Bombay (1988) Mirabai Films. India.
Children Underground (2001) Belzberg Films. Romania.
City of God (2002) Miramax Films. Brazil.
Africa United (2010) Pathe Productions. Rwanda to South Africa.
Street Kids United (2011) Creativity Media. South Africa (Street Child World Cup).

Making sure children get 'HELD'

Ideas and resources to help workers place Hope, Empathy, Love and Dignity at the heart of child protection and support

By Nicki Weld

'Not only are we offered concepts and ideas but clear tools and resources which can be drawn on in day to day practice.' Professor Nigel Parton.

'Passionate, compassionate and persuasive, making a convincing case as to why Hope, Empathy, Love and Dignity are so important . . . provides a number of resources which can be photocopied and used to aid thinking about HELD, gathering information, assessment, planning and intervention . . . informative, inspiring and also practical.' *Well-being*

'A good, strong and engaging workbook that provides indisputably accurate advice and grounded explanations . . . includes worksheets and practical strategies for practitioners to support carers . . . the language is clear and reachable . . . this book holds some gems. This book will appeal to professionals working with carers and professionals alike who are involved in the direct care, support and/or assessment of looked after and accommodated children.' *Child Abuse Review*

978-1-905541-55-3

Safeguarding children and young people

A guide to integrated practice

By Steven Walker and Christina Thurston

'Affirms it is everyone's responsibility to work together to safeguard children.' *Rostrum*

'Packed with resources, case studies and examples to inform you and help you train and equip others.' *Youthwork*

'An invaluable tool for everyone working with children and young people.' *YoungMinds*

'A valuable guiding resource.' *Community Practitioner*

'A wonderfully rich resource.' *Professional Social Work*

978-1-903855-90-4

For more details visit www.russellhouse.co.uk

Personal development matters

A guide and step-by-step educational workbook for helping young people aged roughly 11–16 with complex needs to get to know themselves better
By Kathryn Plant

For use in any context where workers are struggling to adapt mainstream material for teaching personal development in one-to-one or small group settings. Complete with guidance for use, it can be used step-by-step or selectively for specific needs. Ideal for weekly hour-long sessions over the course of a year.

'An excellent tool for enagaging young people.' Dr Jane Toner, clinical psychologist. 'I have already seen noticeable improvements in our young people's self-awareness and understanding of their own emotions.' Liv Hansen, teacher. 'The content is current and flexible, and the provision of a separate student workbook (available for purchase separately) adds a different dimension to other resources of this nature, ensuring ownership, continuity and progression . . . a great resource book for anyone wishing to guide and support vulnerable young people on their journey of self-awareness and discovery. Recommended!' *Youthwork*

978-1-905541-69-0

Young people in foster and residential care

Answers to questions you may be asked by 11 to 18 year olds in your care
By Ann Wheal

'Aimed at carers, care staff and managers in residential settings, and staff supporting foster carers . . . The main emphasis is on guidance and suggestions around the myriad issues likely to be raised by those being looked after . . . This well presented and accessible publication is to be commended for its clarity and sheer practical usefulness.' *Care and Health*

It includes photocopiable checklists and forms that may be useful to the young people.

978-1-903855-27-0

For more details visit www.russellhouse.co.uk

Journeying together
Growing youth work and youth workers in local communities
Edited by Alan Rogers and Mark K Smith

Founded on the view that
- young people are members of communities – now, not at some point in the future
- their voices must be heard, for the benefit of all
- there are leaders in the making amongst them.

'Each chapter is rich with theory and real life testimony shared in stories straight from the frontlines of youth work embedded in local communities. Refreshing, inspiring and utterly convincing . . . calling us to return to long-term investment in local communities where collaboration between funders, trainers and youth work projects enables sustainable, and ultimately, truly transformational youth and community work.' *Youthwork*

'More than anything, the book aims to inspire youth workers and others in the sector to take the talent, ability, excitement and "spark' and use it to innovate further.' *Children & Young People Now*

978-1-905541-54-6

Having their say
Young people and participation
Edited by David Crimmens and Andrew West

'A very useful insight into the development of participation . . . written clearly . . . easy to follow . . . an interesting and informative read for policy makers, professionals and young people themselves, and indeed anyone interested in developing children and young people's participation in political life, citizenship and social inclusion.' *Children & Society*

'The editors provide chapters exploring a theoretical model and an overview of the role of the government. These chapters are followed by nine varied examples of youth participation from around Europe . . . an invaluable and practical tool for anyone charged with ensuring the participation of children.' *Community Care*

'Interesting and informative . . . bringing together ideas on how to make the participation agenda work.' *Youth & Policy*

'Will be beneficial to all policy makers, practitioners and researchers with an interest in enhancing participation for children and young people.' *Adoption & Fostering*

978-1-898924-78-4

For more details visit www.russellhouse.co.uk

The art of youth work
Second edition
By Kerry Young

This valuable resource has been thoroughly revised to examine youth work purpose, principles and practice in the context of changing social and political agendas for young people. It reaffirms its commitment to youth work as an exercise in philosophy, not because young people are troubled or troublesome, but because they are people in the process of reconciling reason and passion in ways that make sense to them. You will find here a:
- clear theory of youth work
- framework for making sound judgements about practice and the training of youth workers
- reaffirmation of youth work, at its best, as a powerful educative and developmental process.

978-1-903855-46-1

The RHP companion to working with young people
Edited by Fiona Factor, Vipin Chauhan and John Pitts

'Covers almost completely the territory which youth work now occupies ... the editors have done a magnificent job ... enables the reader to explore very disparate issues in a systematic way.' *Young People Now*

'Packed with useful material ... the 32 chapters are of a uniformly high standard.' *Community Care*

'Brings a wealth of practical experience and a rigorous critical approach to its examination of the needs of young people and of the different styles of intervention that have been developed to meet those needs.' *Voluntary Voice*

'Get it. Share it'. *Rapport*

978-1-898924-52-4

For more details visit www.russellhouse.co.uk

Leadership
Being effective and remaining human
By Peter Gilbert

'Asserts a powerful and clear image of the human service leader.' The International *Journal of Leadership in Public Service*

'Reminds us that leadership occurs at all levels . . . impressive.' *Nursing Standard*

'The chapter on the use – and potential abuse – of personal power and authority is essential reading . . . suitable for anyone practising leadership at whatever level and provides excellent scope for reflection on personal aspirations and performance.' *Social Caring*

978-1-903855-76-8

Partnership made painless
A joined-up guide to working together
By Ros Harrison, Geoffrey Mann, Michael Murphy, Alan Taylor and Neil Thompson

'Until now there has been no book that sought to give practitioners or managers explicit guidance in how to make partnerships work. This volume seeks to fill that gap . . . it does so admirably . . . an accessible 'how-to-do-it' approach . . . the practical experience of the authors in establishing and nurturing partnerships does give the book the feel of lived reality . . . clear and succinct.' *Vista*

'How refreshing to read a book that goes beyond the rhetoric and addresses some of the problems which can accompany it . . . will be of practical help.' *Community Care*

978-1-898924-88-3

For more details visit www.russellhouse.co.uk